Oxford Sculpture

An illustrated guide and appreciation of a selection of the stone and wooden architectural carvings, church and chapel memorials, monumental brasses, and public sculpture over 900 years from the Normans to the present.

Bibliography and acknowledgements inside back cover

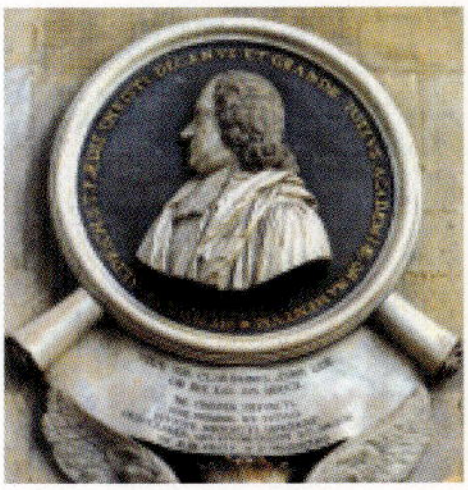
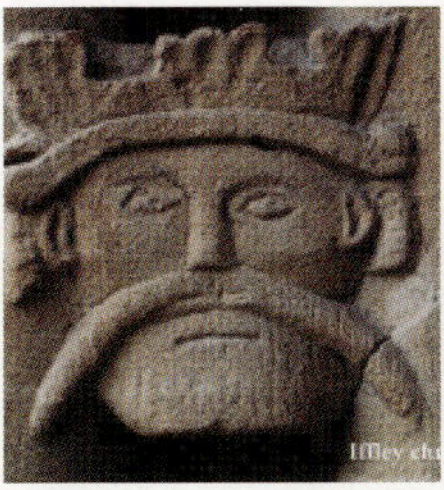
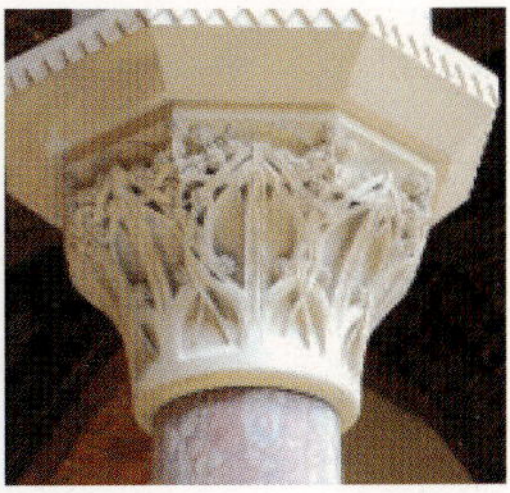

Philip Opher 2009

Heritage Tours Publications ISBN 978-1-874361-27-5

Introduction

Oxford, one of the best-preserved historic towns in England, is rich with eight centuries of ancient churches, venerable colleges, historic streets and buildings – all with their vast, intriguing variety of sculpture that illuminates the culture and events of their various times.

This booklet will help you seek out and enjoy these treasures, most of them in their original settings, performing their original purposes. Through these examples it is possible to appreciate past eras and their artistic achievements, from Norman times up to the present day. The *Oxford English Dictionary* defines sculpture as "the art of forming representations of objects etc. or abstract designs in the round or in relief by chiseling stone, carving wood, modelling clay, casting metal or similar processes": an enormous range of possibilities. Here we show you some of the most interesting work in Oxford, and you'll also have the opportunity to discover many other similar examples as you explore the city.

Sculpture is rarely, if ever, made only as "art". Most commonly, sculpture fits an architectural scheme **(1)**, an overall design in the style of the period in which it was made: Romanesque (usually called Norman in England), Gothic, Classical or Modern. Carvings often serve a spiritual purpose, as an object to worship, to inspire, or tell a story. In the shrine of St Frideswide in the Cathedral **(2)**, and in many different representations of Christ, the Virgin, and the Saints, this function is served. There are sculpted memorials created to recall a person's life, achievements, sometimes even their appearance **(3)**. Statues in public places honour a benefactor, a hero, a monarch — or just 'furnish' a space.

Sculpture, although usually better preserved than contemporary wall painting, is still subject to deterioration, especially where exposed to the weather **(4)**. At various times, sculpture has been destroyed deliberately and much has been lost. Restoration is difficult and often robs the piece of its character, although some re-cut works have a beauty of their own. Despite the ravages of centuries, much that remains is well worth seeking out.

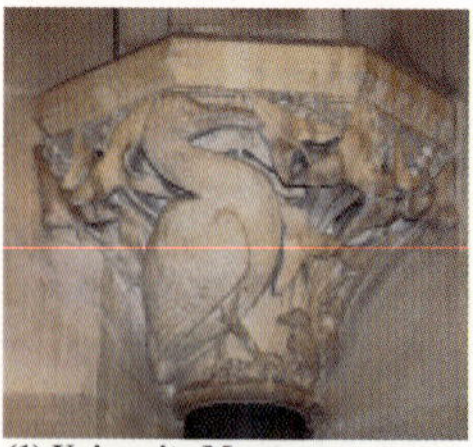

(1) University Museum

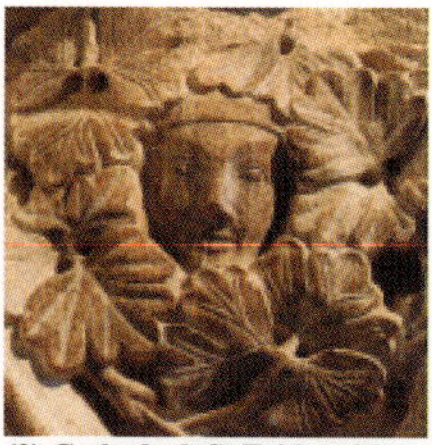

(2) Cathedral, St Frideswide

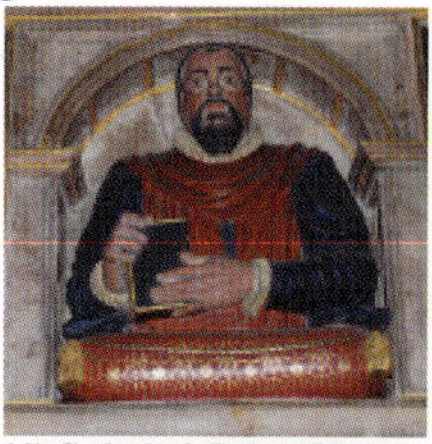

(3) Cathedral, Robert Burton

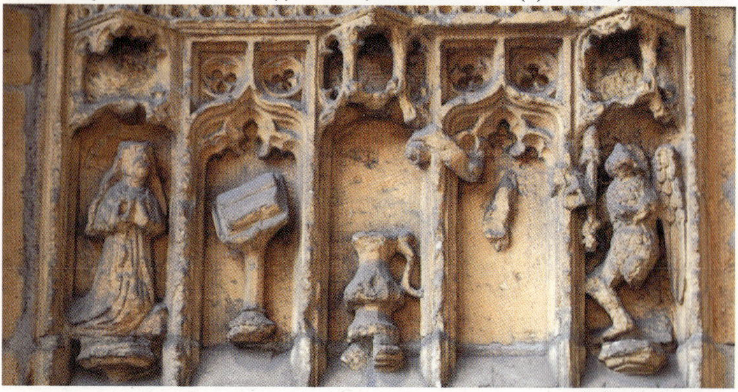

(4) Hertford College

Medieval stone carving

Apart from the wonderful Ashmolean collection (not included in this publication), which has sculpture of all periods from the earliest times, there is very little sculpture in Oxford dating from before the Norman invasion. But from 1066 onwards, there are plenty of excellent examples of medieval work. The best carvings are in the cathedral and on the lovely little church of St Mary's at Iffley, both built during the 12th century. Throughout the middle ages, and especially during the Romanesque period, the Roman Catholic Church, as an international organization, set the style and subjects of carving over a wide area, with masons travelling from place to place to carry out commissions. Early work is sometimes unsophisticated but illustrates a love of geometric forms, elaborate patterns derived from illustrated manuscripts and, above all, of natural and mythical beasts. These subjects were chosen to decorate the house of God, inspire in the illiterate population a love of God's creation (and sometimes warn against sin) and tell them the Christian story.

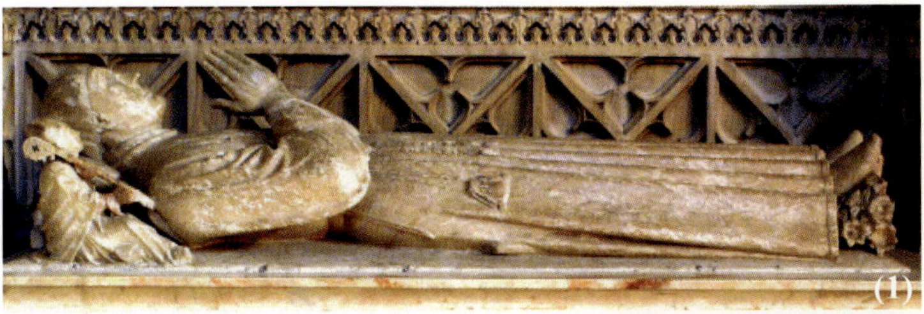

As the Gothic style slowly evolved during the 13th and 14th centuries, there was as increasing amount of architectural sculpture and a change in the composition and subjects of the images. These changes resulted in a greater abundance of natural foliage and more graceful, realistic figures; examples in the chapter house and on the shrine of St Frideswide in the cathedral illustrate these changes. Good examples of this style, known as "Decorated", can be also being seen on the lovely tombs in the Lady Chapel of the cathedral. The chief glory of medieval Oxford came during the 15th and early 16th centuries, the so called "Perpendicular period". The Patten tomb at Magdalen College **(1)** the ceiling vault of the Divinity School **(2)** and the Zodiac vault at Merton College **(3)** are among the best examples in England. A host of figures, saints, monarchs and patriarchs in the reredos behind the high altar at All Souls, at New College and at Magdalen, although largely restorations and without the colour and gildings common to all medieval sculpture, still gives an idea of this rich flowering of medieval carved art. The period came to an abrupt end when the monasteries and their masons' yards were closed in 1540 and the Iconoclasts of the Reformation set about destroying religious images.

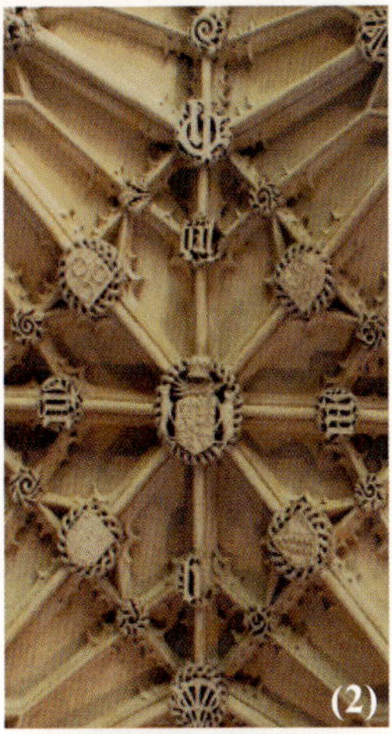

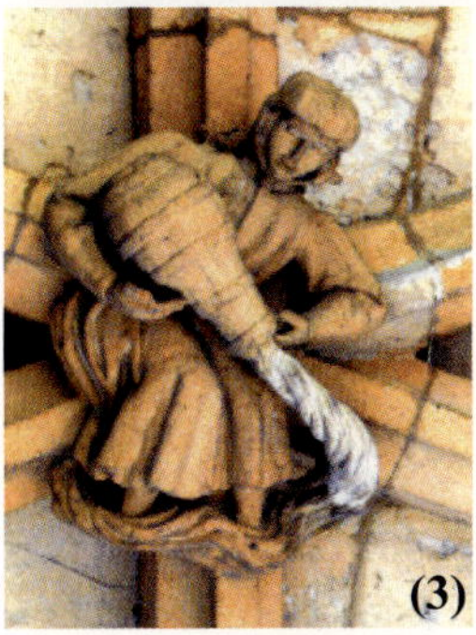

Medieval wood carving

Oxford has fine examples of medieval wood carving, although much was destroyed during the Reformation and the Civil War. Medieval church furnishings were sparse, concentrated on the stalls for the priests and choir. The bench ends of these stalls were sometimes decorated with abstract designs or figures known as "**Poppy Heads**". Oxford's best examples are in the Latin chapel of the cathedral. There is also a fine collection of **Misericords** under some of the stall seats in college chapels. The seats are hinged, with a small ledge underneath. Elderly (or lazy) priests, tired during the long services, could squat on this ledge while appearing to remain standing. These strange small-scale carvings are generally religious but include other themes of medieval life and beliefs, sometimes grotesque or even erotic. Misericords (from the Latin *miserere,* "have mercy") can be seen in the antechapel at Magdalen College **(1)**. It is usually possible to see a few of the fine examples at New College. But the best collection, at All Souls, can be studied only with special permission.

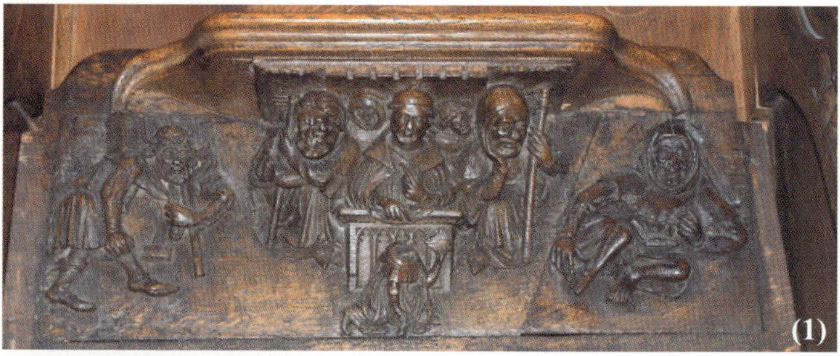

(1)

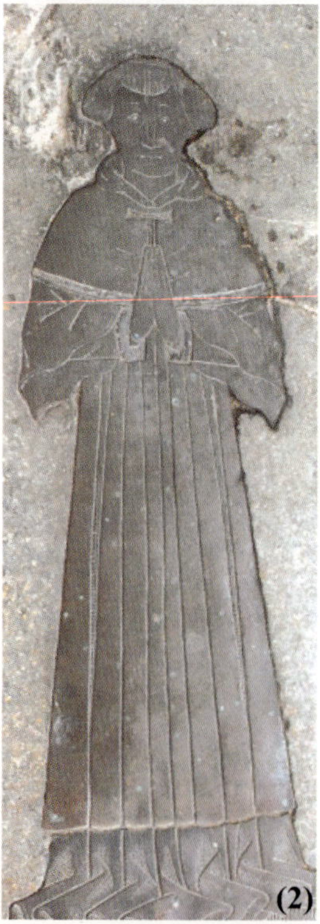

(2)

Medieval monumental brasses

A few good examples of the medieval craft of brass engraving can be seen on the floors, or occasionally on the walls, of religious buildings in Oxford. These relatively cheap memorials started to appear in the 13th century and developed as a particular English artform until the 16th. Figures, usually slightly less than life-size, and generally standardized, are not realistic portraits, but they do give an accurate representation of the costumes of the period. In Oxford most of the brasses are of the clerics who taught in the university. Brasses can be found in most ancient Oxford churches and at Merton **(2)**, New College, and Magdalen. The memorials became a source of cheap scrap metal during the Reformation, when Iconoclasts destroyed "graven images". It is still possible to see shaped indentations in the floor slabs of some church floors where the brass was ripped out, to be melted down to make armaments. A few brasses that were removed survived and their reverse side reused for a later memorial. There is an interesting example of this, a 'palimpsest', in the north transept of the cathedral.

Medieval grotesques

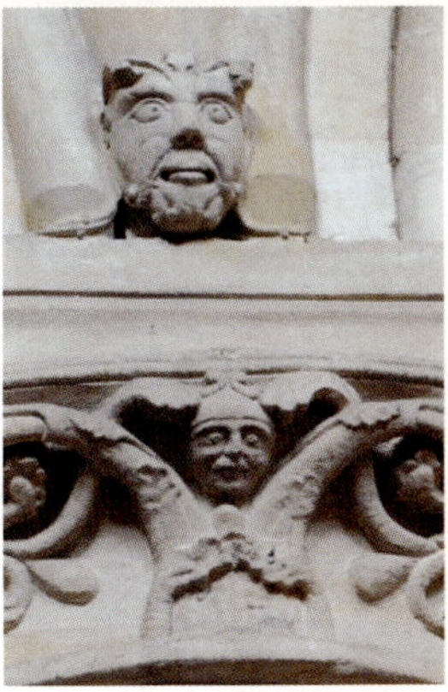

Carvings of strange beasts, mythical or real, and of distorted human forms, sometimes caricatures of real people, are a curious feature of medieval art. Although they are usually found in churches, grotesques have no clear religious significance and are often hard to interpret. Apart from their incorporation in misericords and bench ends, they are usually high up on corbels or along a string course. Modern versions, occasionally with the faces of contemporary people, can be seen on restored buildings

Renaissance sculpture

The Protestant reforms during the reign of Henry VIII were accompanied by the slow assimilation of the ideas of the humanist Renaissance from Europe, which began to influence the style and content of all forms of British art. The rediscovered vocabulary of classical details was used by artists right up to the 20th century, with variations to accord with changes of fashion. The earliest Renaissance carving in Oxford, a modest affair with garlands and plump cherubs, can be seen below the oriel window in the south tower of Cardinal (Wolsey's) College, now called "Christ Church". Apart from this panel and some minor monuments, Oxford has little Elizabethan sculpture. During the whole of the 17th century, however, despite the disruption caused by the Civil War and the Commonwealth in the middle years, many excellent memorials were created in the cathedral and in college chapels, with the Bodley and Savile memorials at Merton College leading the way in 1613 and 1632. Religious imagery has completely disappeared at this time, replaced by life-like representations of the deceased, surrounded by symbols of their achievements, by classical elements, garlands, swags of leaves and flowers, urns, cherubs, and the architectural orders. New materials, particularly coloured marbles and alabaster, are used, although painting and gilding soon died out. From this period on it is possible to identify professional artist/sculptors, unlike the anonymous medieval masons. Individual public sculpture also started to appear during the 17th century, both in stone and bronze. *Le Sueur's* statue of the Earl of Pembroke in the Bodleian quadrangle is the best known example in Oxford. Classical elements, more realism, and richer use of decorative devices can be seen on monuments throughout the Baroque, Rococo, and neo classical styles of the 18th and 19th centuries.

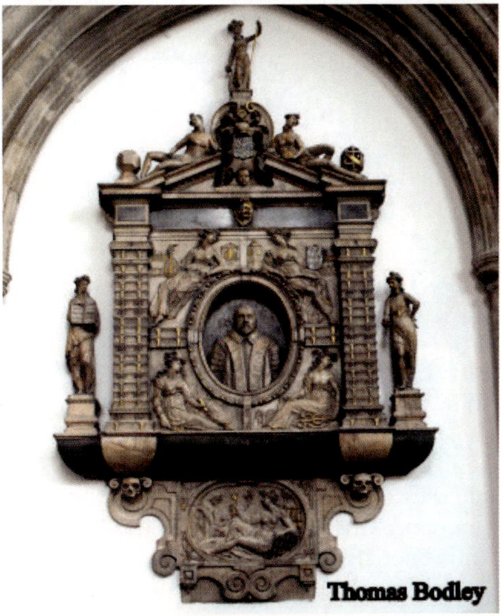

Thomas Bodley

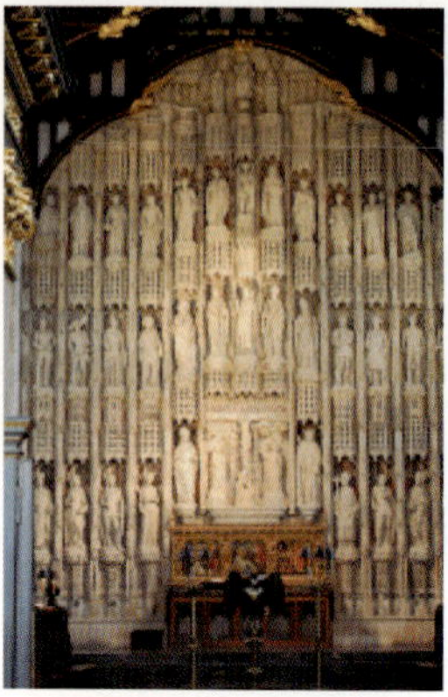

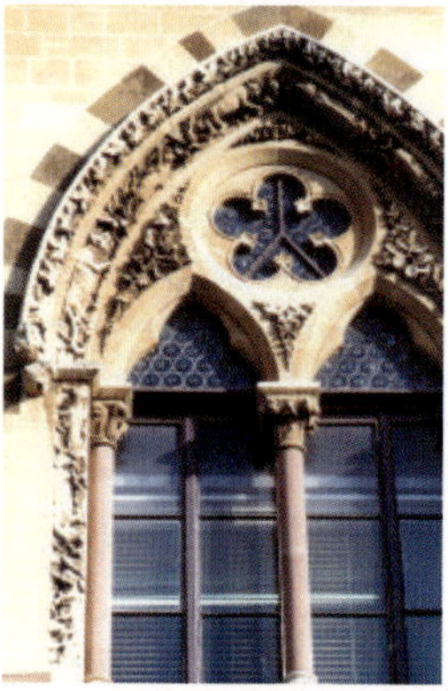

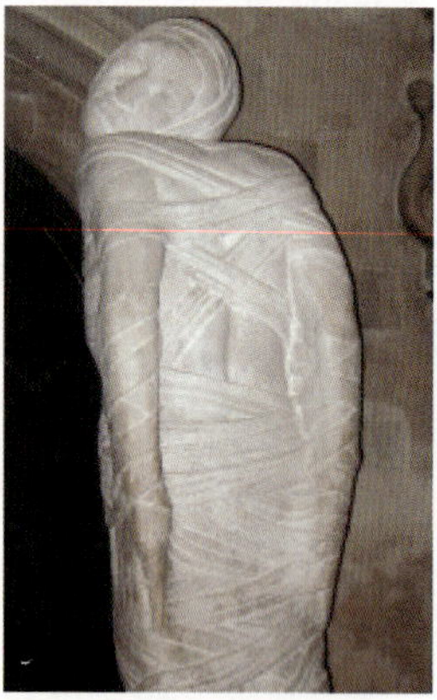

The Gothic Revival

Oxford, which never completely abandoned an attachment to the medieval, was an early and enthusiastic supporter of the Gothic revival, influenced and encouraged by Oxford scholar John Ruskin, the Pre-Raphaelites, and the "Oxford (neo-Catholic) Movement". The wonderful original work of the O'Shea family in the University Museum was inspired rather by the spirit than the forms of medieval work, while the magnificently restored reredos behind the altars at New College, All Souls, and Magdalen were intended as copies of 15th-century originals. The Gothic details architects designed and masons carved on many of the large Victorian university buildings greatly exceed Oxford's original medieval works.

Modern Sculpture

Twentieth-century sculpture is not well represented in Oxford but there are a few pieces of interest, both abstract and figurative. Elaborate memorials went out of fashion and the functional architecture style of the second half of the century did not encourage sculptural embellishment. International Modernism introduced abstract forms, which predominated elsewhere, but conservative Oxford preferred the stylized - but still realistic - work - of artists such as Eric Gill. His commissions included incised "Stations of the Cross" in the modest church of St Alban's in east Oxford and carved wooden doors in the Radcliffe Science library. One of the most famous of all the sculpture in Oxford is Jacob Epstein's masterpiece, 'Lazarus', in which the figure is shown bursting from his shroud. This work is brilliantly sited in the antechapel at New College, proving that it is possible to integrate work in a contemporary style into this ancient city, where there is always the temptation to go back to tradition.

The Gazetteer

In the following gazetteer, some of the most interesting sculpture from all periods is illustrated and briefly discussed. There is plenty more for the discerning eye to discover in Oxford. The places listed here are on a suggested route round the city and can be located from the map inside the back cover. Generally locations and entrance information is indicated in red. For memorials and tombs the date of death is indicated with †, the name of the sculptor, where known, is in *italics*..

St Mary's Church Iffley

Church Way Iffley. The church is usually open.

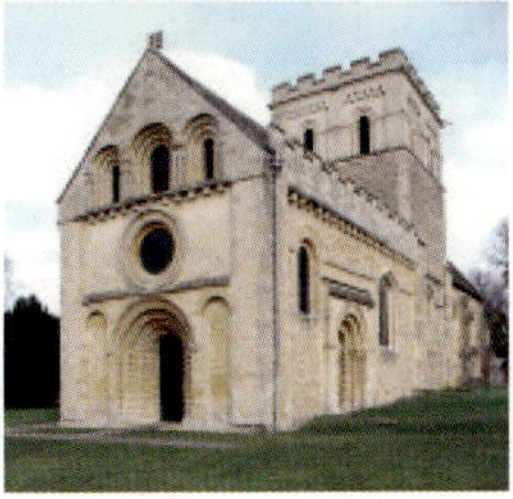

Anyone interested in early stone carving must visit the wonderful Norman (Romanesque) church at Iffley, one of the best preserved in the country. Visitors will also enjoy the two-mile stroll along the river (starting from the south side of Folly Bridge), the opportunity to rest in The Isis, one of the most pleasant riverside pubs in Oxford, and get glimpses of the lovely village of Iffley. Iffley church was built towards the end of the 12th century. The building has been sensitively restored several times but remains much as it was when originally constructed. As in all medieval churches, the whole building is a massive piece of carved masonry. Note especially the Norman sculptural decoration round the west and south doors and, inside, the carvings round the two massive arches beneath the tower.

West door

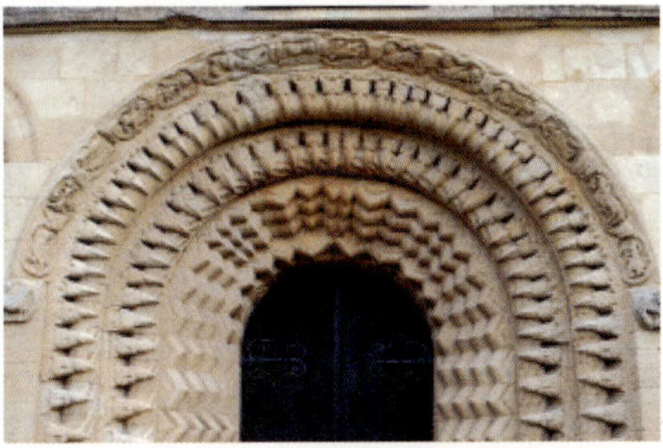

The principal door into the church, this has wonderful beakhead and zigzag decorations carved round its semi-circular arch. There are four continuous bands (orders): four rows of deeply-cut chevrons, two rings of beakheads and on the wonderful outer ring, cartouches joined by lion heads. Signs of the zodiac, symbols of the Evangelists, and mythical animals are, from left to right, an eagle with scroll, Aquarius, Pisces, a winged bull (St Luke ?) an angel (St Matthew ?) a dove, Jonah and the whale, another dove, a winged lion (St Mark ?), a winged ox, an eagle, a seraph, and two monsters.

South door

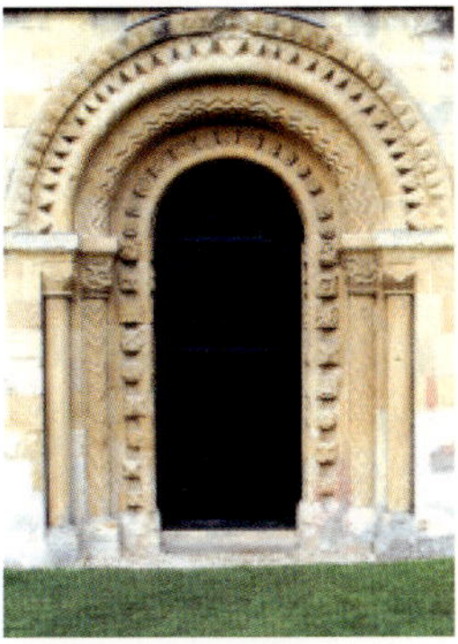

The surrounds to this much smaller door are the chief glory of the church, better preserved by a porch, removed in the 19th century. Although the iconography seems strange today it was common in the twelfth century. The carving was probably done by itinerant masons, based at the large abbey in Reading, who were familiar with models from northern France. The west capitals illustrate centaurs and beasts and a lion attacking a horse. On the east capitals, mounted men fighting, and Samson and a lion. The inner order has carved rosettes, leaf designs, heads of a man and a king, monsters, a lion, a sphinx, a merman, and a bird.

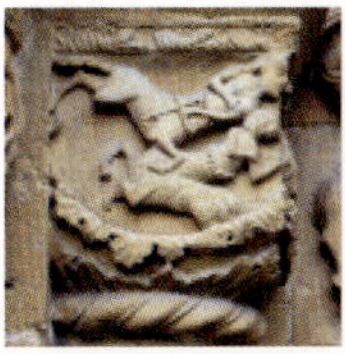

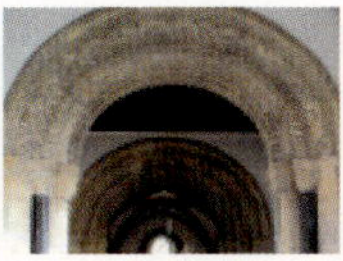

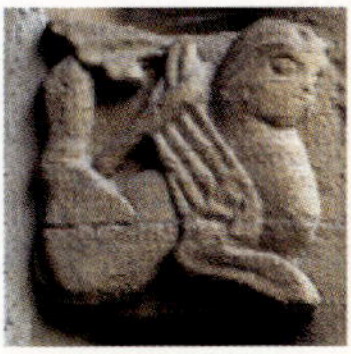

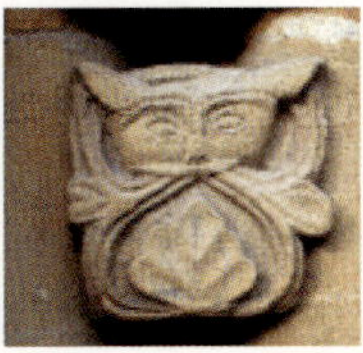

The interior

The massive, monolithic, undecorated stone font, just inside the west door, is an impressive piece of carving, but the eye is immediately drawn towards the raised east end and the two semi-circular arches supporting the tower. The decoration on both these arches is similar: two bands of deeply-cut zigzag chevrons and large, stylized lotus flowers on the outer ring. There are some delightful details, including a bird sitting on her nest. The central boss at the junction of the vaulting ribs combines a strange monster and lions' heads. The whole effect is superb.

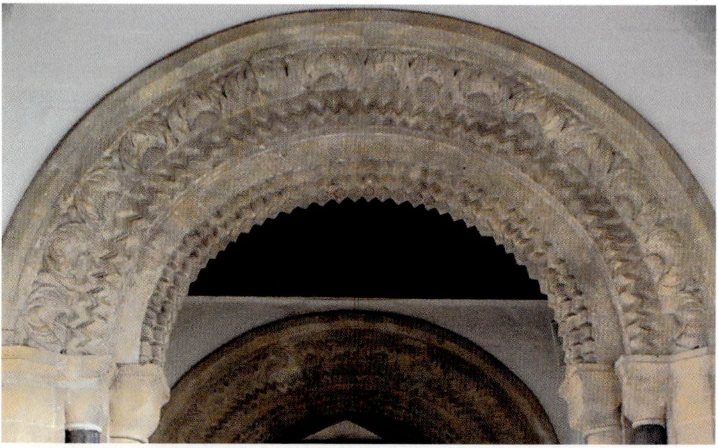

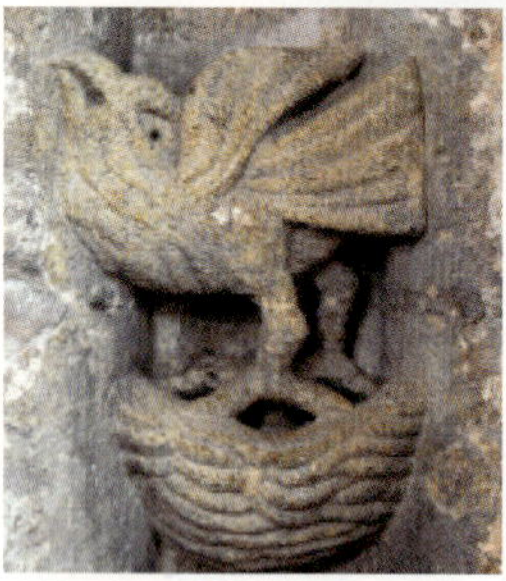

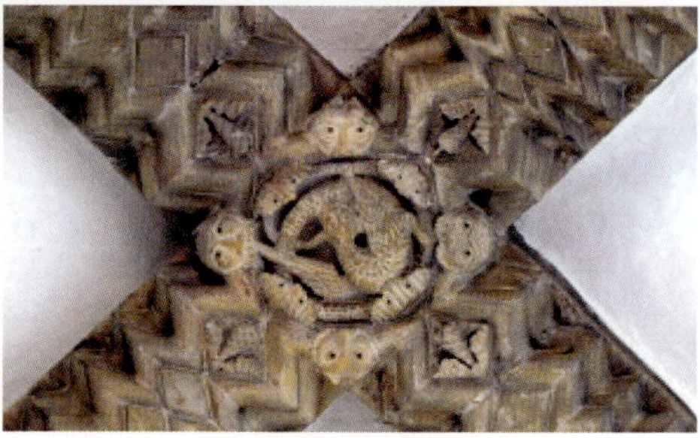

Christ Church, The College and Oxford Cathedral

Parishioners can obtain a free pass to enter the cathedral via the main gate, other visitors must pay a fee to enter through the Meadow building daily 9am-5.30pm Sunday 1pm-5.30pm last entry 4.30pm

The Cathedral Chapter House The Cathedral Shop.

The Chapter House, entered from the cloister through a Norman door that remains from a previous building, is an elegant example of early Gothic design, built at the beginning of the 13th-century. Column capitals, corbels from which the vaulting springs, and the wonderful keystone bosses at the junction of the ribs of the roof are all excellent examples of the developments of Gothic carving. The bosses illustrate Christ, the Virgin and Child, St Frideswide, and a lion with one head and four bodies.

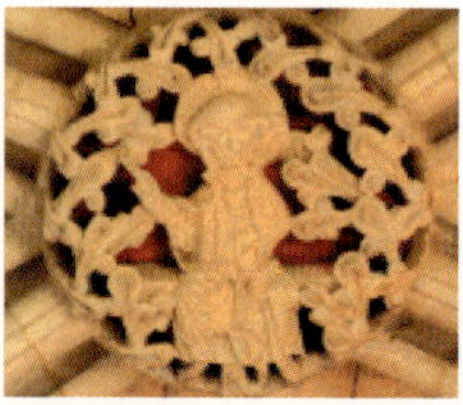

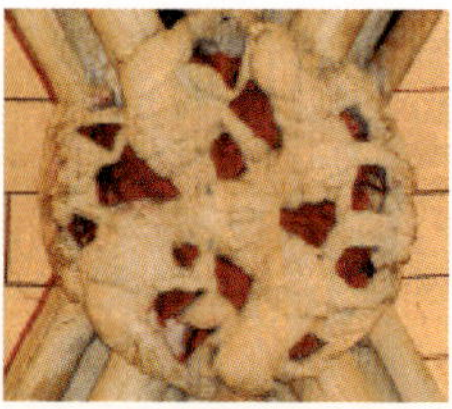

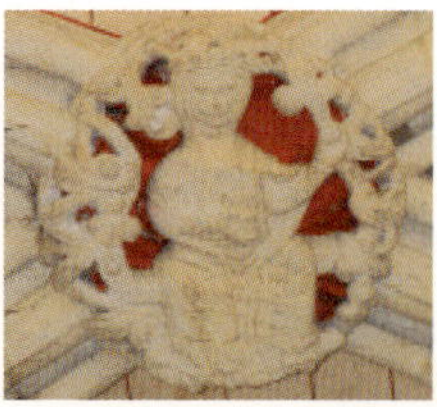

Oxford Cathedral, embedded in Oxford's grandest college, has a wealth of interesting architectural decoration, several splendid tombs, some good poppy heads on older stalls (fixed seats), nearly 100 wall monuments and some fine pieces of sculpture.

Medieval carving

The majority of the building is late Norman; massive, plain, and robust. Detailed decoration is rare, confined to the capitals of huge cylindrical columns. No two capitals are exactly the same; some have intricate patterns derived from illuminated manuscripts, others have crockets and leaf-forms. Above the capitals there are some grotesques which can be seen best through binoculars.

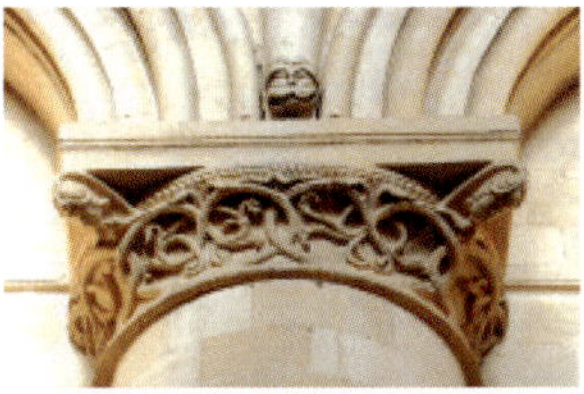

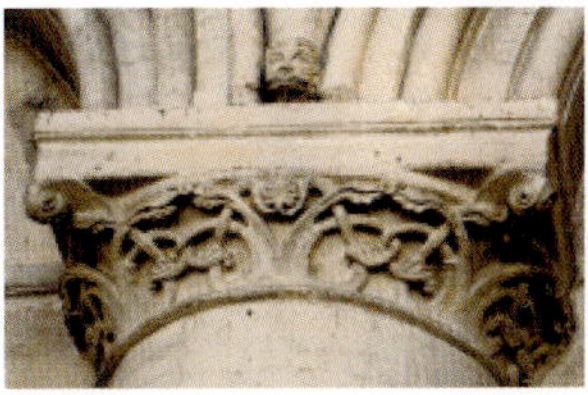

Latin and Lady Chapels

These two chapels were added on the north east corner of the cathedral in the early Gothic period. The keystones have some interesting carvings and there is a rich collection of shrines and tombs from the 13th and 14th centuries. The Sutton, Montacute, and Nowers tombs provide an interesting spectrum of three major aspects of 12th-century life.

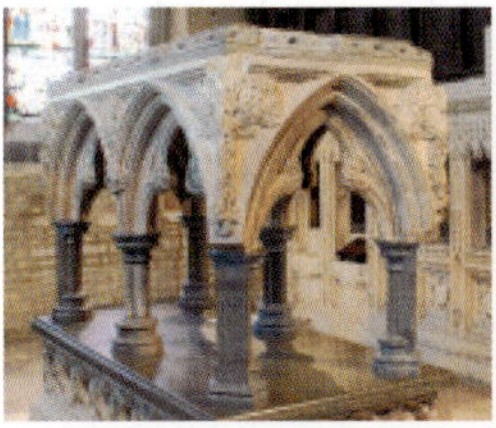

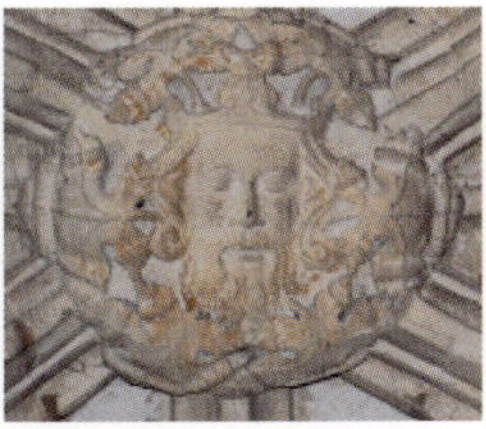

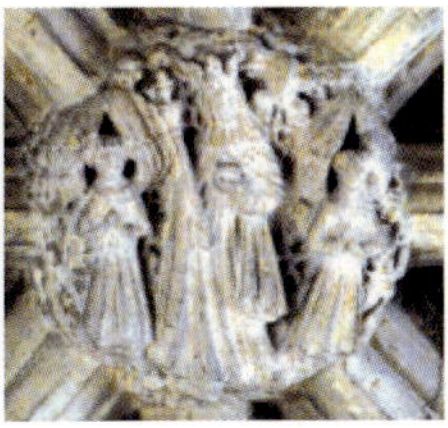

Saint Frideswide Shrine Latin Chapel

The best examples of early Gothic carving are the fragments of the shrine of Oxford's patron saint. Carved in 1289, destroyed at the dissolution of the monasteries, it was recently reconstructed. The mysterious female faces peer through naturalistically rendered foliage. It is exciting to get close to such wonderful craftsmanship and identify the finely carved details: natural leaf and plant forms, oak, ivy, and vines.

Elizabeth Montacute †1354 Latin and Lady Chapels

The full-length marble figure has a beautifully delicate embossed dress and a typical hair-style of the period. Elizabeth's dog is at her feet and on both the sides of the tomb-chest there are delicate figures of weepers (mourners), one man, one woman, and three nuns on the north side, and two men, a bishop, and two women on the south side.

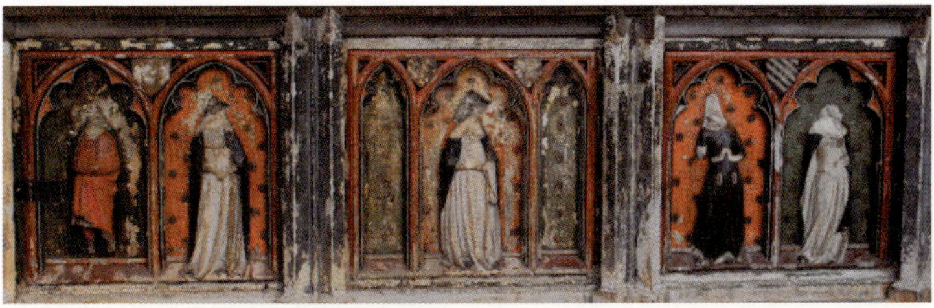

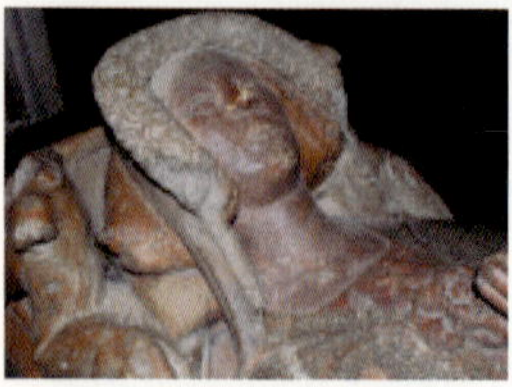

Sadly, the Puritans decapitated the figures, but the costumes retain their grace and beauty. Elizabeth was married twice, hence she has Montague and Furnival shields of arms. The well preserved original colouring gives a good idea of how all medieval sculptural monuments would have looked when new.

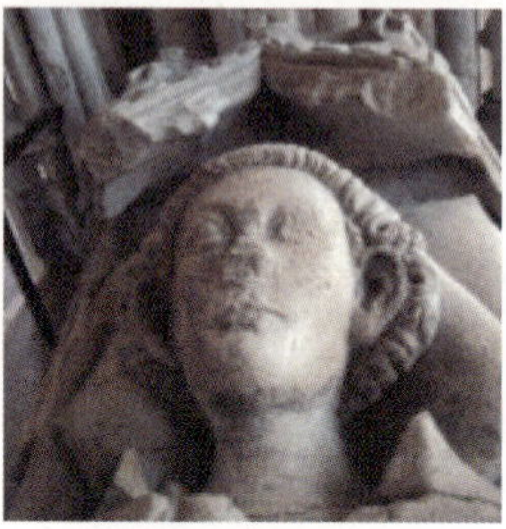

Prior Sutton †1316 Latin and Lady Chapels
A miniature "Decorated Gothic" building, with three gables and a cluster of black Purbeck marble shafts, houses the full-length figure of the Prior in the vestments of the Mass. His head is shaved and his feet rest on a lion, a symbol of the Resurrection. Although stylized, this is an early medieval realistic portraiture, an art form that had faded after Roman times.

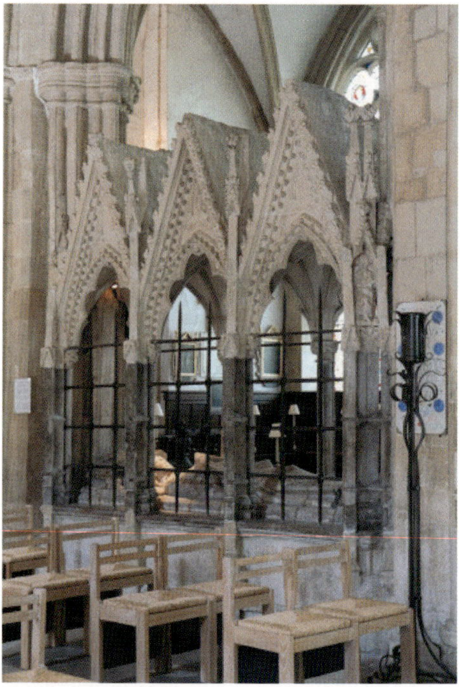

John de Nowers †1386 Latin and Lady Chapels.
This alabaster tomb is the only example in Oxford depicting a knight in full armour, sword in hand, legs crossed, his feet resting on a dog and his head on an ox. Apart from the badly repaired nose, the face and figure escaped the worst attentions of the vandals.

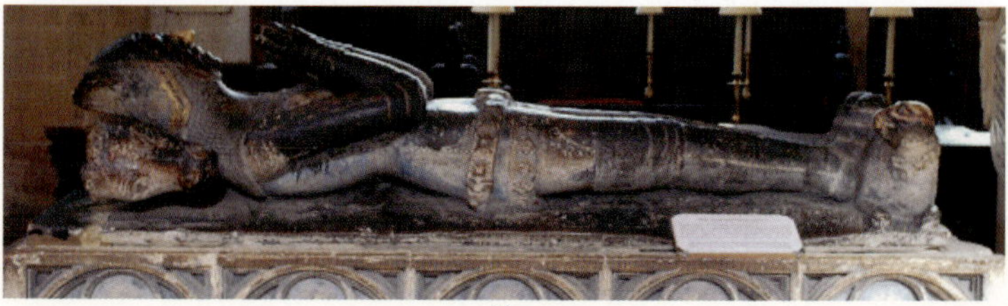

Poppy heads Latin Chapel.

The stalls in the Latin Chapel include some of the best wood-carvings in Oxford, equal in quality to the misericords at New College and Magdalen College. Called "poppy heads", these are in fact small carvings of foliage, a cardinal head, angels, and grotesque heads. They have no purpose except to delight, illustrating the stylistic exuberance of 14th century craftsmen.

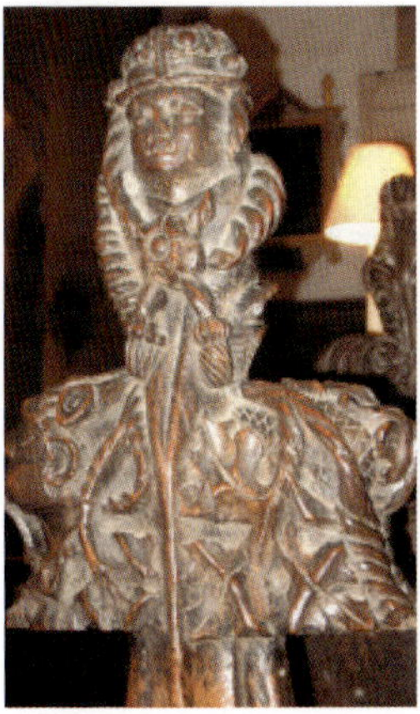

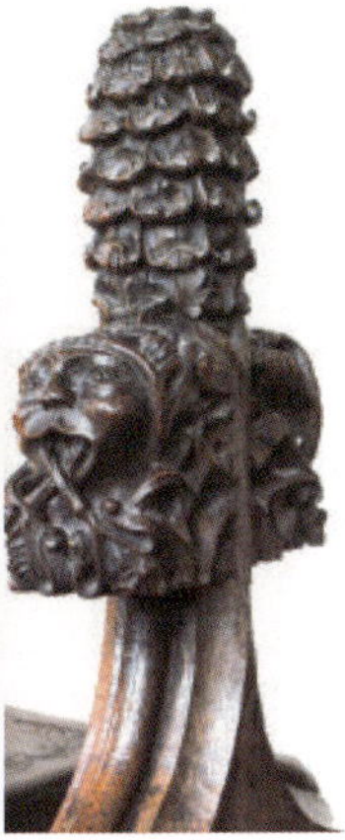

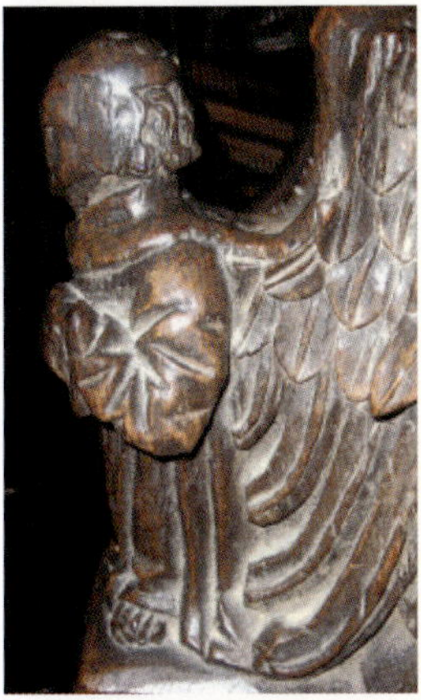

Brasses

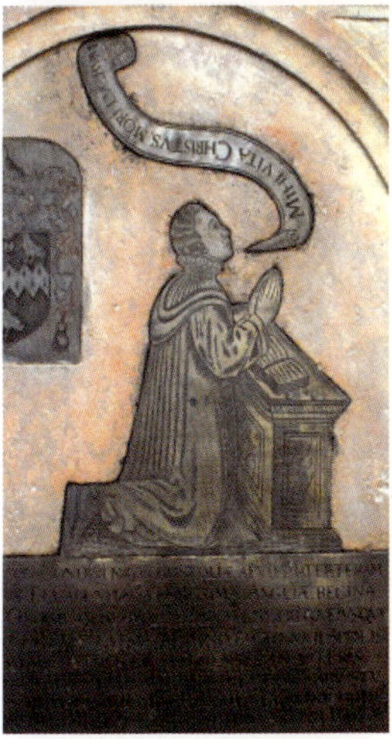

Very few of the cathedral's medieval brasses survived the Civil War. The indentations from which they were ripped, to be turned into armaments, can be seen in the floor. Two small brasses, to **John Fitzalyn †1452** and **Edward Courtney †1462**, survived, badly worn. A much larger one, to Frederick Barnes, is 19th-century Gothic Revival. The most fascinating brass is a small wall plate to **Henry Dowe †1578** in the north wall of the north transept, one of the first memorials created in the cathedral after the Reformation. The plate is a palimpsest, part of a 14th-century brass monument which was turned over and re-used. An explanation alongside illustrates the large head on the reverse.

The Choir (Chancel) **Vault**

This stunning 15th-century lierne vault, the work of William Orchard (see Divinity School), has beautifully carved pendants and bosses at the junctions of the vaulting ribs. Along the central ribs there is a head of Christ, a Virgin and Child, St Frideswide (?) flanked by angels, an archbishop and a bishop. Where the vault joins the tower, canopied niches frame life-size figures of St Mary Magdalene and St Peter (?) on the north side, with St Katherine and St Paul (?) opposite. These are probably earlier than the vault itself and escaped destruction during the Reformation. Earlier still are two 14th-century corbels of male figures, one playing the lute.

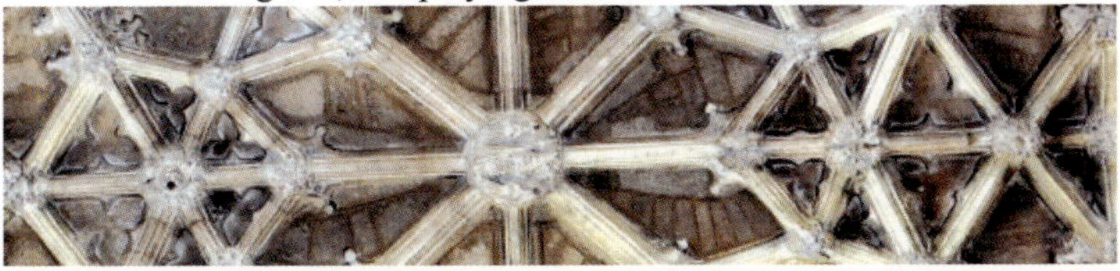

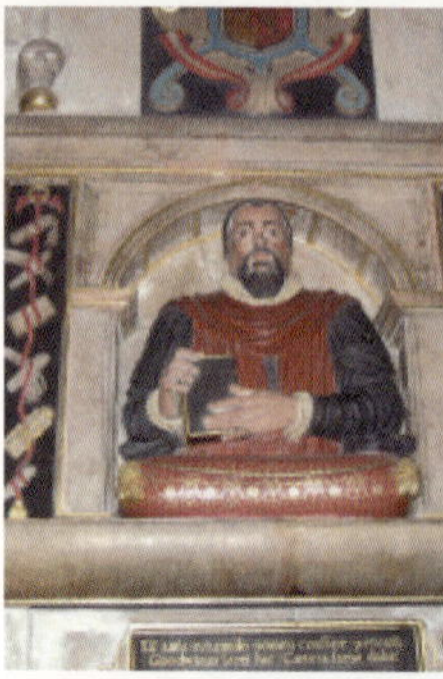

(1)

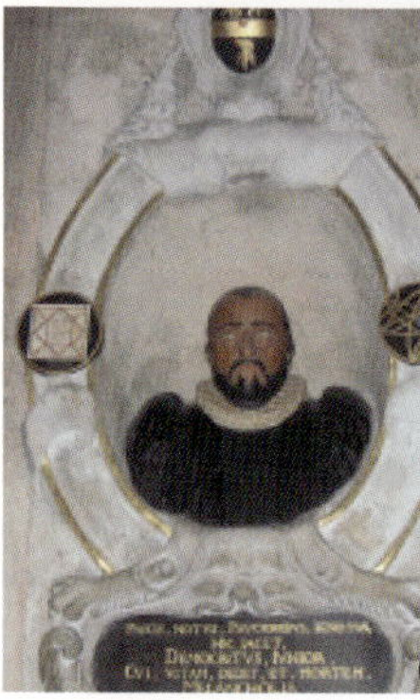

(2)

Renaissance monuments

The Renaissance was not fully established in Oxford until early in the 17th century, but by the time Charles I moved here with his courtiers in the 1640s, during the Civil War, masons and sculptors were familiar with classical forms and details. Many of Charles' supporters died and were buried in the cathedral, together with the great and the good of later times. The walls are lined with their numerous memorials. There is only space here to detail a selection of the best, with a list of some of the others at the end.

William Goodwin †1620 (1) and Robert Burton †1639 (2) North Transept East Aisle

Two early 17th-century 'scholar' monuments high up on adjacent piers in the aisle illustrate the complete break from the medieval tradition. Once religious imagery was suppressed during the Reformation, monuments became a statement of man's social position. Here, both figures are realistic portraits, in fairly natural poses, brightly coloured, shown from the waist up, eyes wide open, staring heavenwards, in elaborate frames. Burton's book *The Anatomy of Melancholy* is still read today.

Peter Wycher †1643 (3) South Transept *William Byrd of Oxford*

A form of monument, common during the 17th-and 18th-centuries, known as a "cartouche" (framed scroll). The Wycher monument is a beautiful piece of carving in black and white marble. It has a pair of weeping putti (figure of a child or cupid) on either side of an urn, with another pair of happier putti guarding the Wycher coat of arms.

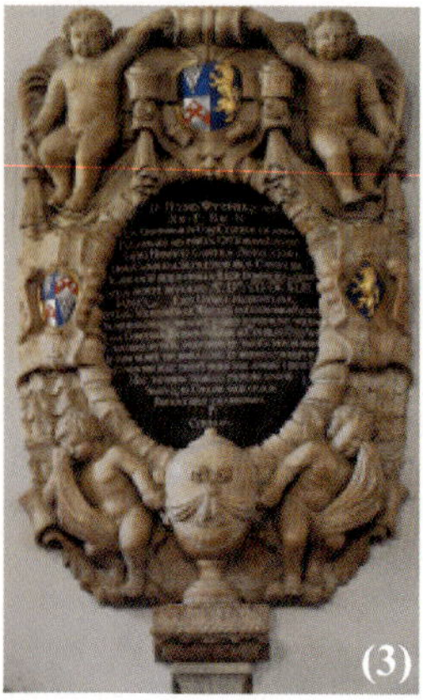

(3)

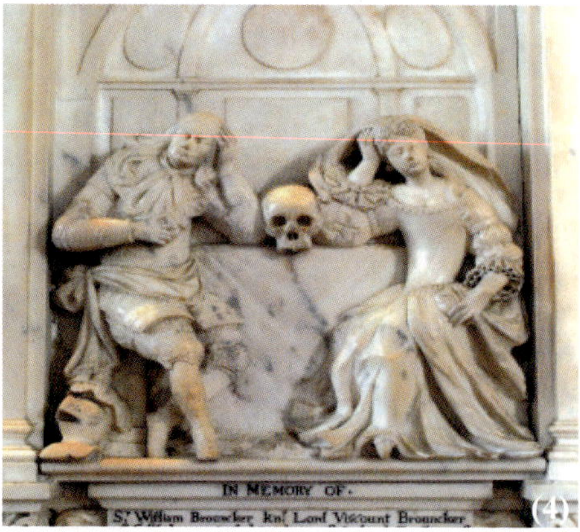

(4)

Brouncker Monument †1645 (4) South Transept

On this unusual, macabre marble monument, husband and wife, separated by a skull, sit brooding over death. The main figures, in high relief, are surrounded by putti keeping guard. The monument was carved by an unknown sculptor. The architectural background is strictly Classical. The sculptor was influenced by late Roman monuments, which often illustrate married couples, although usually in a jollier pose. Brouncker was a Privy Counsellor to Charles I.

Viscount Grandison †1670 (1) South Transept *John Latham*

A beautiful, simple monument consisting of. a splendid, sumptuous trophy urn on a high plinth wreathed in finely carved foliage.

Lord Mounslowe †1645 (2) South Transept One of the most spectacular monuments in the cathedral, with a large pedestal urn garlanded with flowers, perched on an untidy pile of discarded armour. The long biographical text is typical of the period, as are the Classical architectural decoration and black marble sarcophagus. Mounslowe was a Judge and adviser to Charles I.

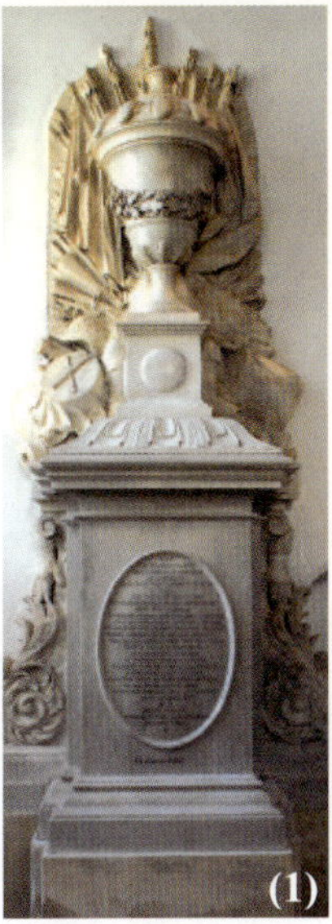

(1)

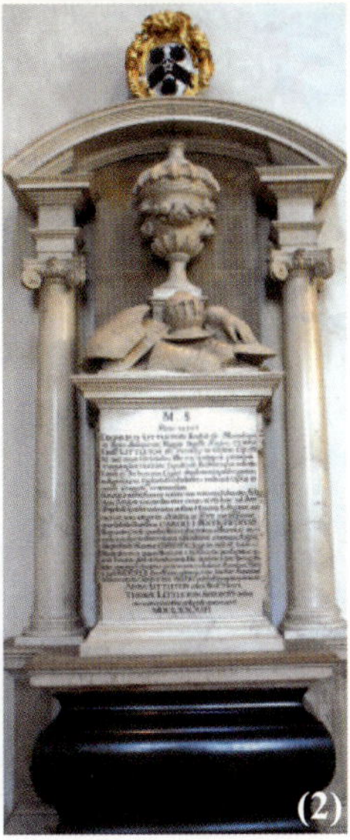

(2)

Edward Pocock †1691 (3) South Nave Aisle

The beautiful bust on a large pedestal high up on the wall has Pocock, wearing a mortar board and cap, staring into the unknown. He was an Oriental Scholar, "the greatest Arabist of all time," also fluent in Hebrew and Syriac: one of the earliest Englishman to have a sympathetic understanding of Islamic religion and culture

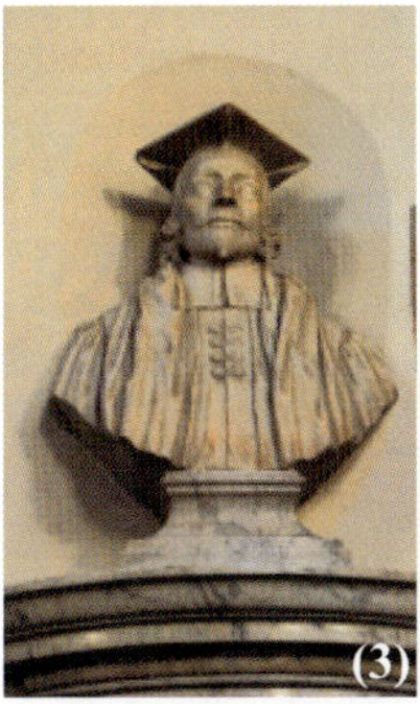

(3)

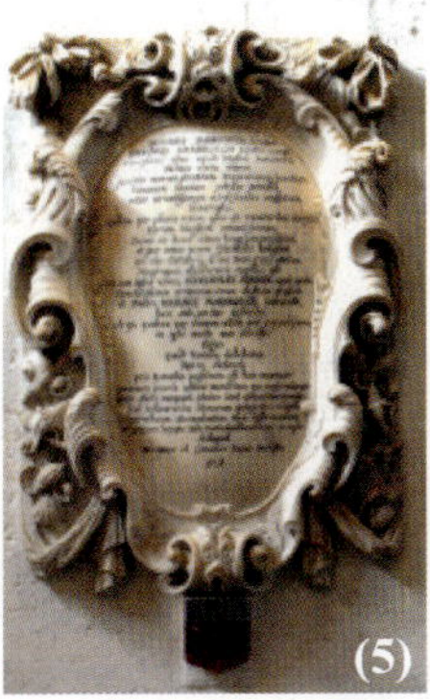

(5)

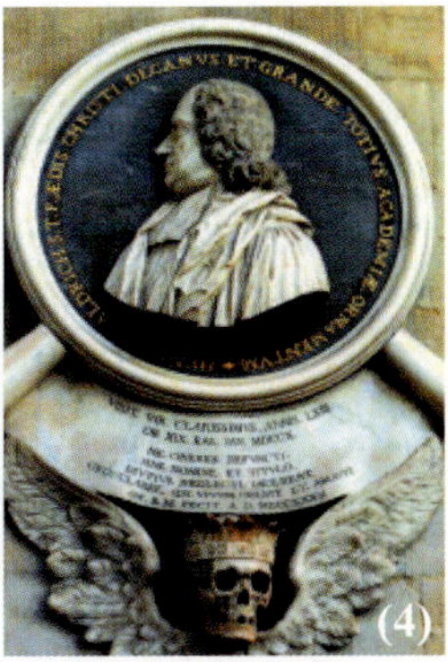

(4)

Dean Aldrich †1710 (4) Nave *Sir Henry Cheere*

The monument has a finely carved half figure in roundel on a blue background. Below the roundel and an inscription on a scroll there is a skull and a pair of wings. Aldrich was a polymath–Vice Chancellor of the University, mathematician, amateur architect (Peckwater Quad, and All Saints Church, ‹now Lincoln College Library›) humourist, drinker, pipe smoker and musician.

James Narborough †1770 (5) South Nave Aisle *William Townsend*

The monument is an elaborate, beautifully carved marble cartouche by William Townsend. The deeply-cut scrolls and the details of sea shells (he died in a shipwreck off Sicily) and natural forms are well worth studying.

George Berkeley †1753 Nave

The excellent wall monument has a sarcophagus with an epitaph by Pope. Above it there is a coat of arms, palm fronds and a bishop's crosier mounted on a black obelisk. Berkeley was Bishop of Cloyne and a distinguished philosopher.

Elizabeth Acland †1878 South Choir Aisle *Alexander Munro*

The beautiful profile of Elizabeth as a young woman is on a pink marble background. Mrs Acland started a training college for nurses as part of the Acland Hospital, founded by her husband Dr Henry Acland.

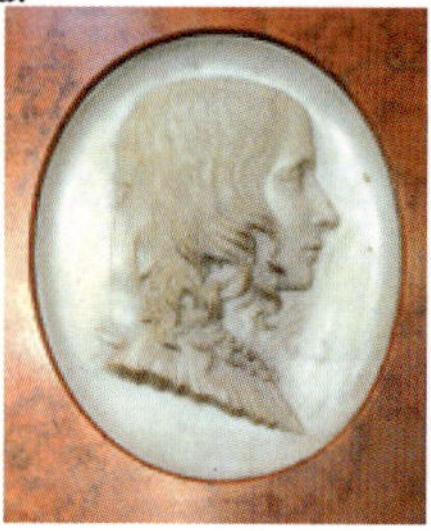

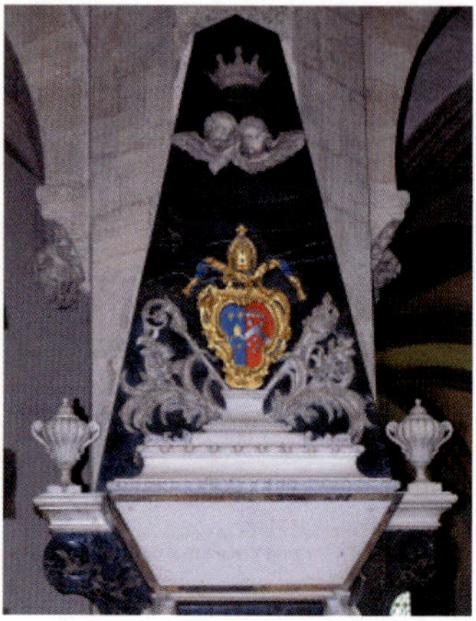

Christ Church, the college

The college, founded by Cardinal Wolsey in 1525, uses the cathedral as its chapel (Wolsey's plan for a magnificent chapel on the north side of Tom Quad was never realised). The first early Renaissance carving in the city is under the oriel window at the far end of the St Aldate's façade. The seriously weathered statue of Cardinal Wolsey, by Francis Bird, is outside Tom Tower. It was made in 1719 but put here only in 1872. On the quad side of the Tower the figure is of Queen Anne. The best known statue at the College, in the Mercury fountain, is a modern copy of a piece by *Giovanni de Bologna*, with a pedestal by *Edwin Lutyens*. The statues on the Bell Tower above the hall staircase and, opposite, on Fell Tower, are 19th century.

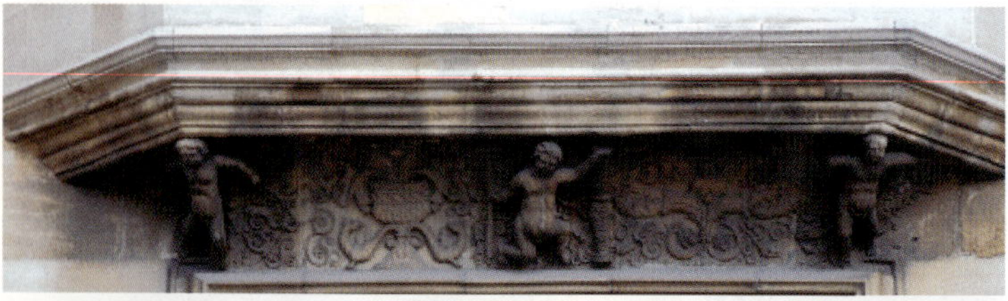

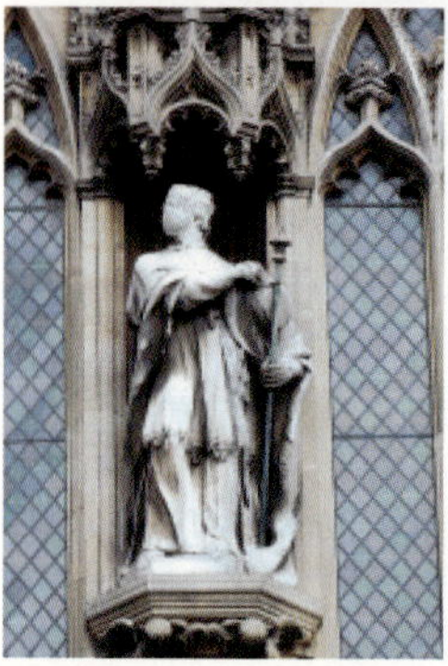

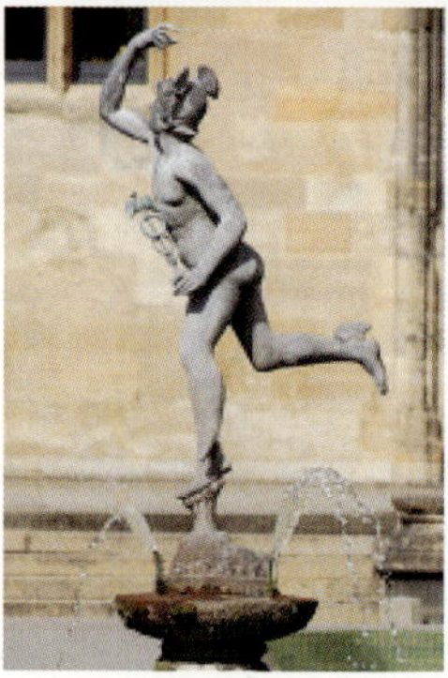

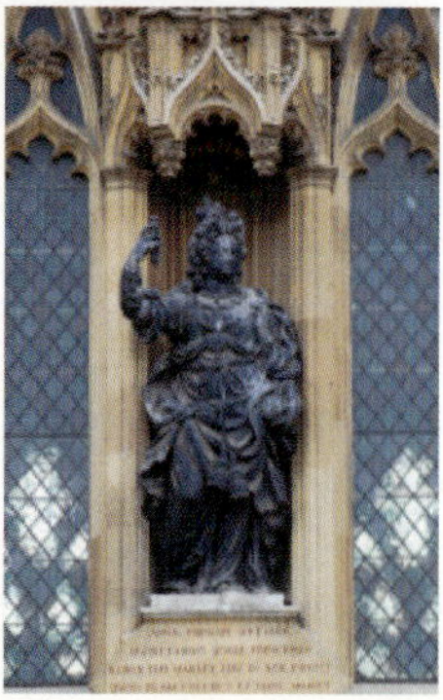

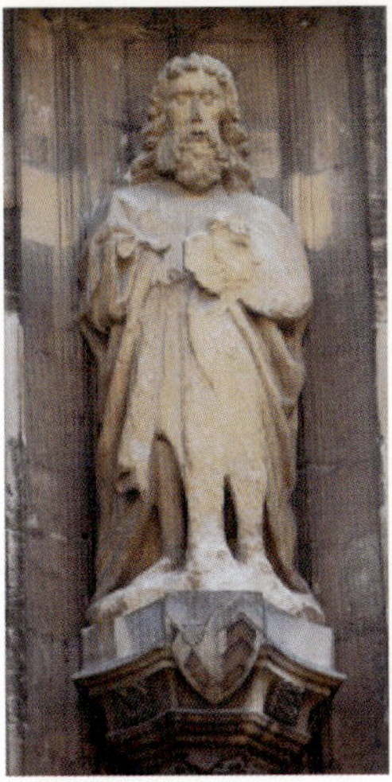

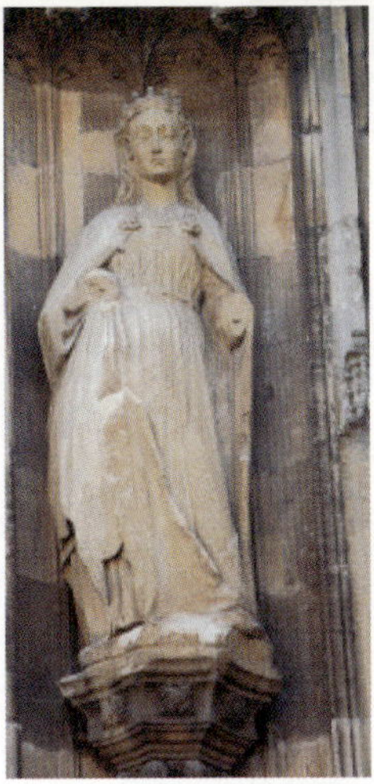

Merton College

The college is usually open in the afternoon

Merton has a rich collection of sculpture. On the north wall of the anti-chapel facing the street there are two original late 15th-century figures (protected with a limewash coating): St John the Baptist, the college patron saint, and the Virgin

The Gatehouse

Further along Merton Street, above the college entrance, the niche figures of the Founder, Walter de Merton, and King Henry III are modern copies, but the delightful small panel below, with lovely details of plants and animals is medieval. The scene shows John the Baptist in the wilderness with the Founder and various animals. The panel was commissioned in 1465 by Warden Sever.

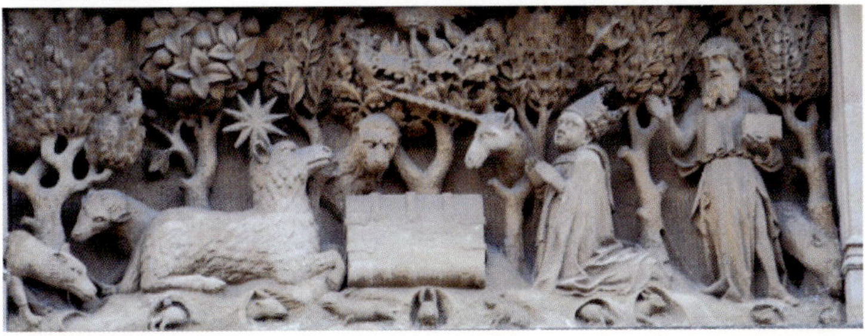

Fitzjames Gateway

Warden Fitzjames was responsible for the eponymous gateway to Fellows Quad of 1497. The lierne vault has a complete set of zodiac symbols, beautifully carved in high relief on the keystones. They surround the Tudor coat of arms with supporters of a dragon and a greyhound. These are some of the best work of the period and a great treat for lovers of medieval sculpture.

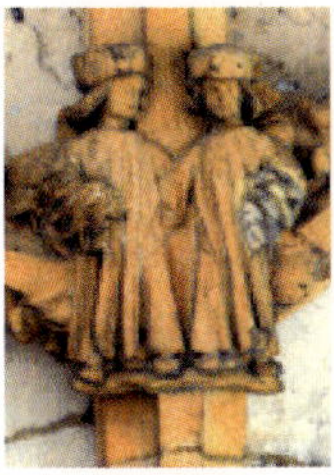

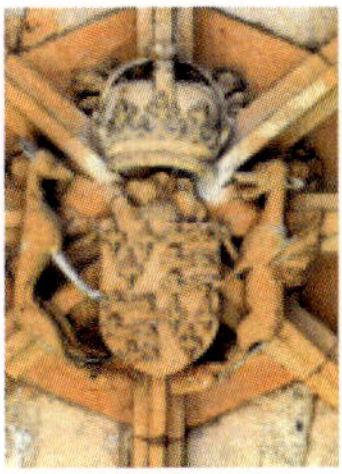

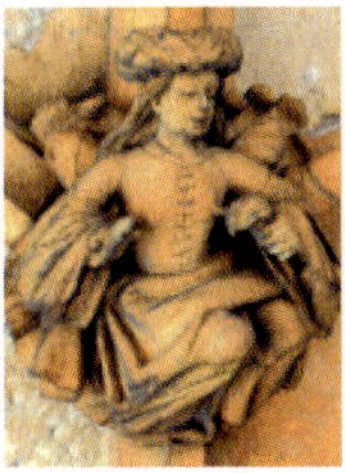

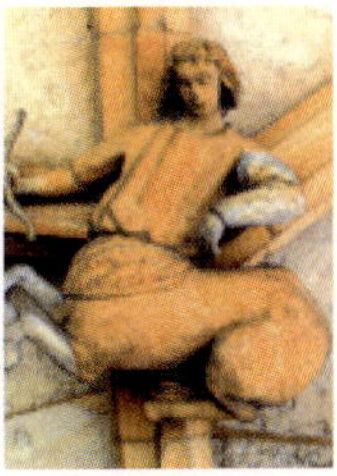

The Chapel

There is another treat in the chapel for those who like early 17th-century monuments. These, and several interesting later monuments, are in the antechapel, together with some good medieval memorial brasses.

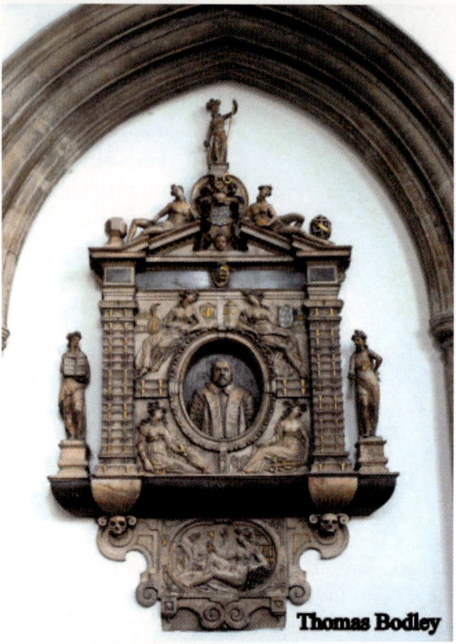

Thomas Bodley

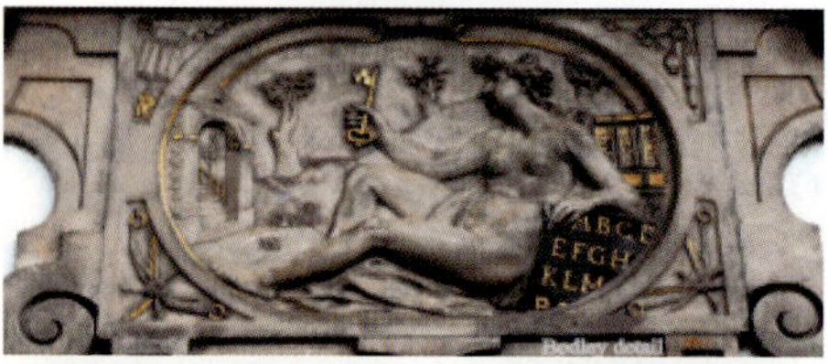

Bodley detail

Thomas Bodley †1613

Nicholas Stone

The splendid wall monument to the founder of the Bodleian Library is on the northwest wall. This is the first major monument in Oxford which has a portrait of the deceased surrounded by secular, rather than religious symbols,which celebrate the life and work of a Renaissance man. There is a three-quarter bust of Bodley in the central oval recess, surrounded by female figures representing Music, Arithmetic, Grammar, and Rhetoric. Piles of books form the pilasters on either side to support the pediment on which further allegorical figures are perched. Two more female figures stand free on either side. Below all this is a figure, representing Grammar, in low relief, framed in a cartouche.

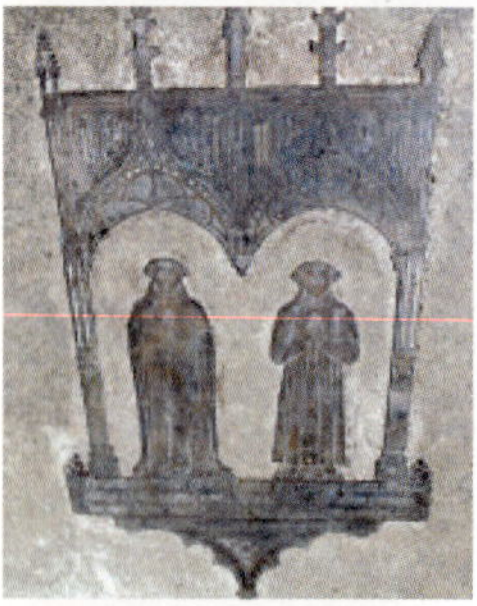

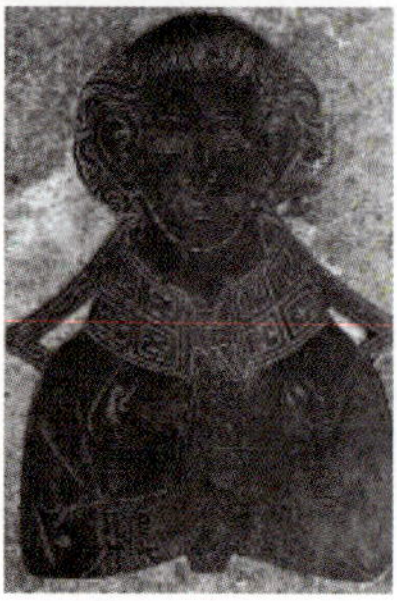

Brasses

Several of the Merton brasses survived the scavengers and are grouped together in the northeast corner of the antechapel. They include a pair of figures, **John Whitton** and **John Bloxham** on a pedestal surrounded by a canopy and a memorial to Warden **Richard de Hakebourne**.

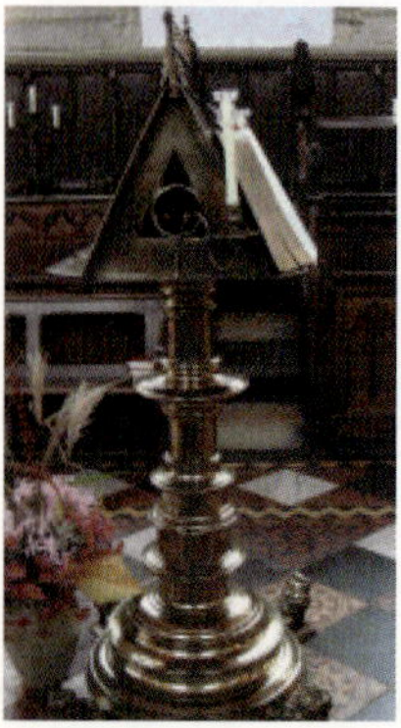

Lectern

There are several splendid brass lecterns in college chapels. The one in Merton Chapel, from the early 16th-century, is one of the best in Oxford. Standing in the middle of the choir, the magnificent casting has a reading desk on each side incorporating the arms of Warden Fitzjames. Other interesting lecterns are in Magdalen and St John's Colleges.

Warden Henry Savile †1621

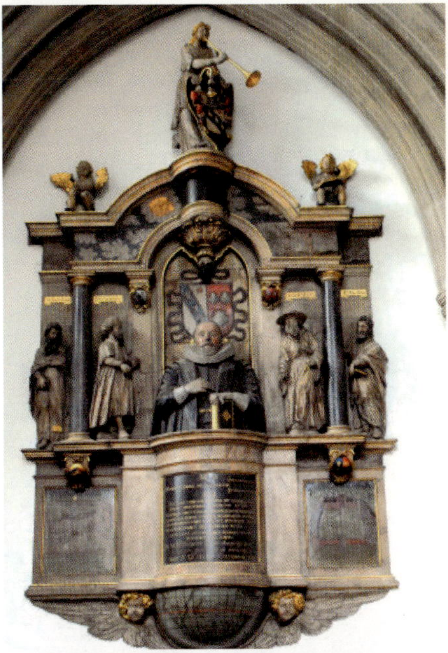

The monument, to the distinguished Warden, on the southwest wall of the antechapel, rivals Bodley's in its magnificence and imaginative use of Renaissance motifs. The three-quarter bust is flanked by standing figures of St John Chrysostom, Ptolemy, Euclid, and Tacitus, arranged either side of a pair of Doric columns. Two cherubs sit above an elaborate curved pediment with the figure of Fame blowing her trumpet on top. Two painted panels at the base of the monument show Merton and Eton Colleges, where Savile was Provost.

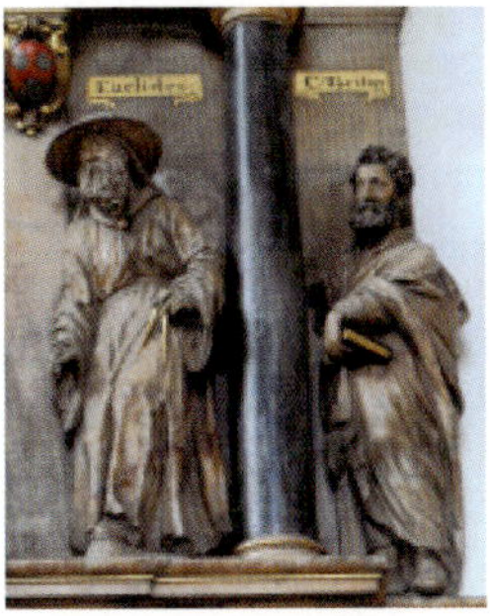

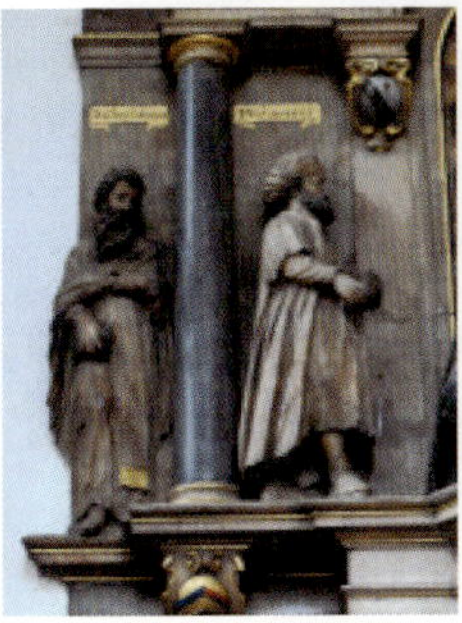

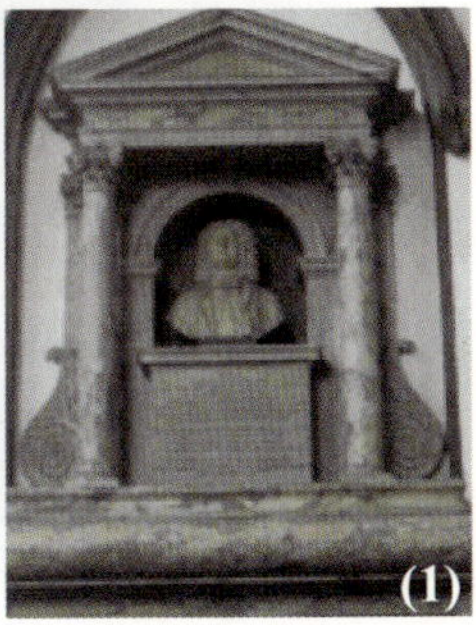

Other monuments

There are several other interesting memorials in the antechapel, including: **Henry Jackson † 1727 (1), Nathanel Wight †1682 (2), Anne and Robert Wyrtle †1750 (3),** a lovely white marble urn with graceful female figures on either side, all framed in a light green marble oval. **Coleridge Patteson †1871 (4),** *by Woolner*, the figure is shown alive at the top and lying dead below. He was a missionary bishop in the South Pacific, killed by a native's arrow as a protest against forced labour in Australia.

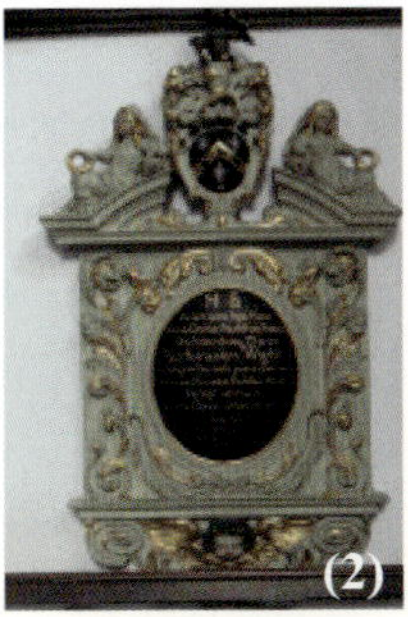

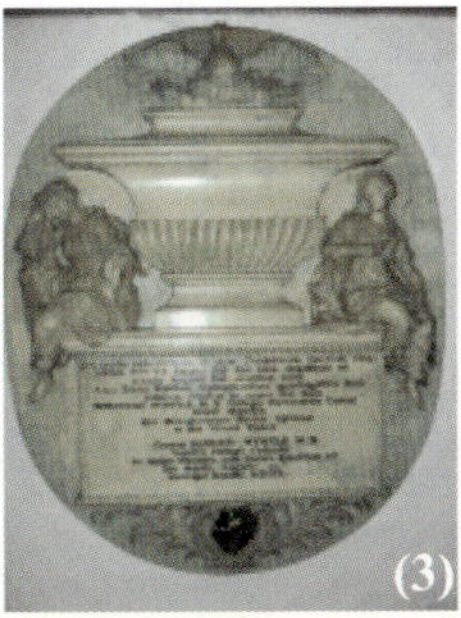

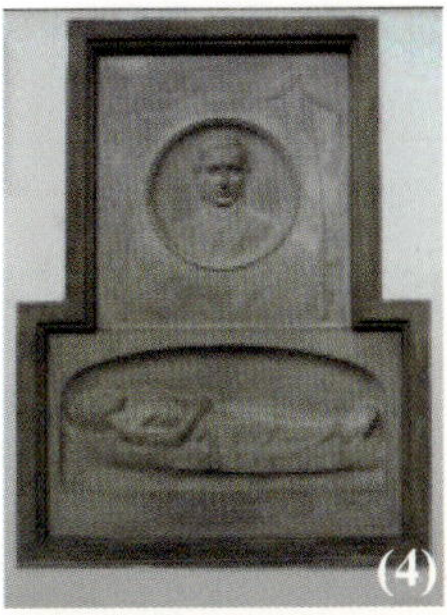

 The Church of Saint Mary The Virgin

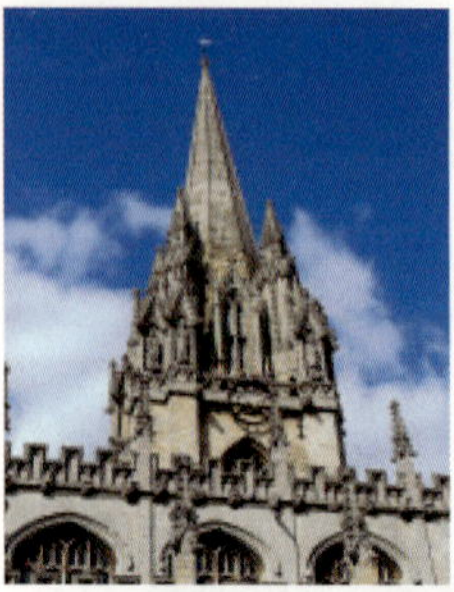

Walking down Oxford's most famous street there is a delightful and rewarding experience for sculpture seekers. St Mary's has a spectacular early spire of 1325, lavishly adorned with decorative pinnacles and covered in ball-flower ornament, a wonderful example of medieval high spirits. The life-size statues of the Evangelists on the bottom corners of the spire were replaced in the 19th-century. The original medieval figures, much weathered, are now in New College cloister.

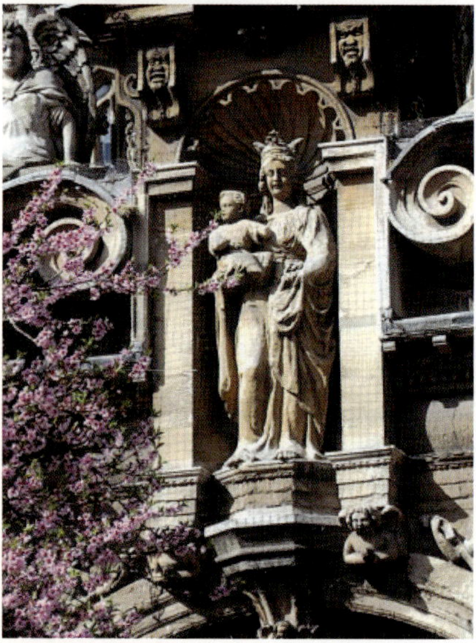

Church Porch

The statue of the Virgin and Child, the centrepiece of the voluptuous baroque entrance porch *(Nicholas Stone 1637),* provoked controversy soon after it was built just before the Civil War. It was used as evidence of his Catholic tendencies at the trial of Archbishop Laud, whose chaplain had commissioned it. Laud was condemned and executed. During the Civil War the heads of both figures were removed (shot off by a soldiers musket ?) but were replaced at the Restoration.

Interior South Aisle Here there are two scholar memorials by *William Townsend:* **David Gregory †1710,** Mathematician and Astronomer, shown in a bust, wearing a full wig, over a panel with cherubs holding a telescope and **John Wallis † 1703,** Mathematician and Cryptographer, with a half-figure, lecturing above a scrolled panel showing a robust female resting on a globe. In the opposite aisle **William Jones† 1794**, a judge in India, with a figure on the left resembling Gandhi.

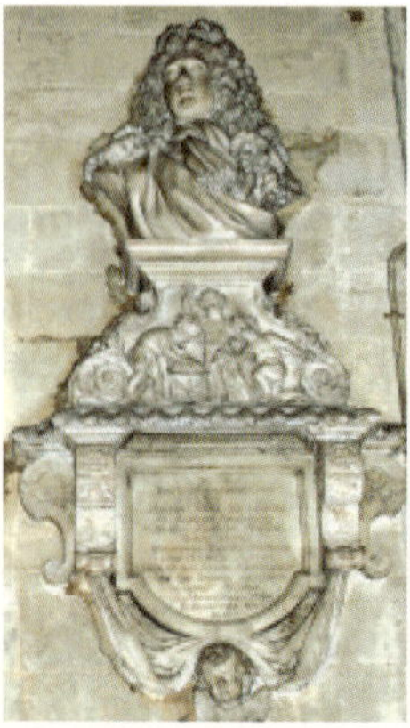

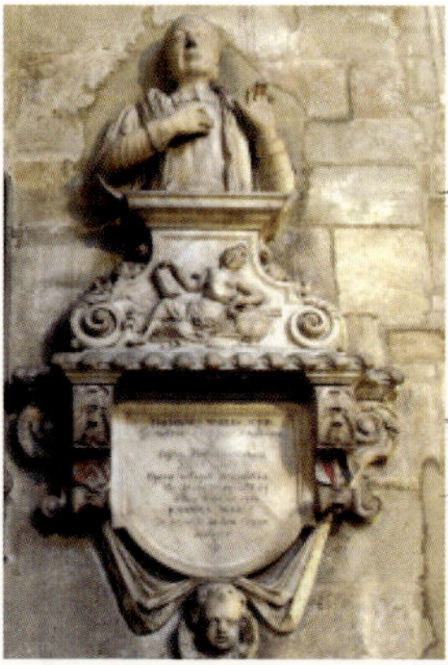

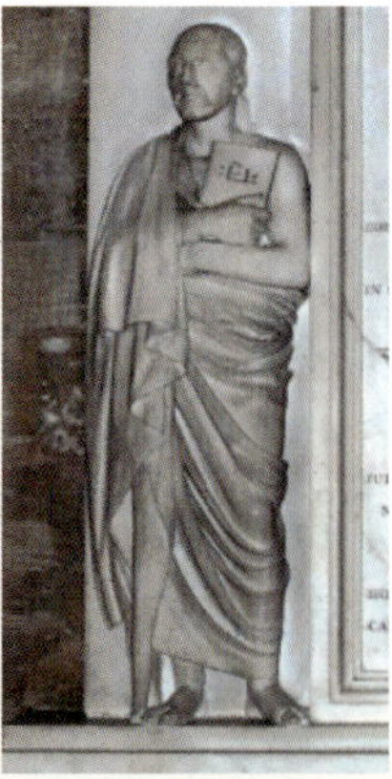

All Souls College The college is usually open in the afternoon 2-4pm

All Souls is a very special Oxford institution comprising Fellows and visiting Fellows promoting the advancement of research,teaching and the maintainance of links with public life. The figures on the High Street façade are modern; the middle one in the style of Eric Gill, by *W.C.H.King*. The worn but still beautiful originals are in the antechapel.

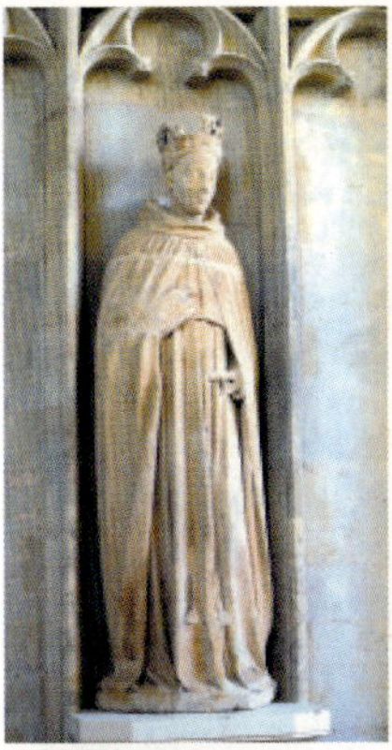

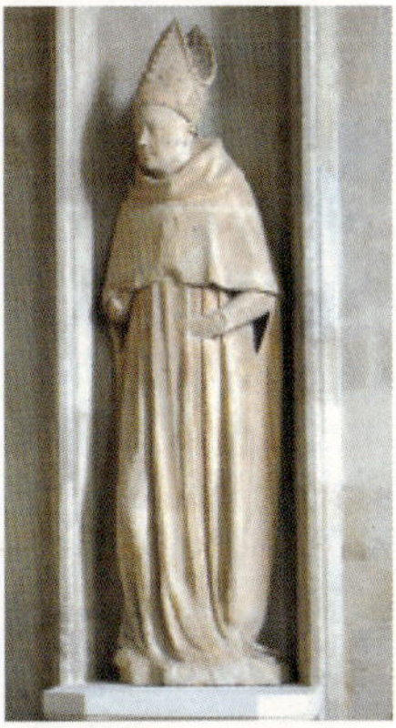

The Chapel

The chief interest in the chapel is the marvellous reredos which fills the eastern wall. The whole impression is a riot of late medieval exuberance. Although the figures are Victorian by *E.C.Geflowski,* the framework of uprights and the back are original of 1447. The figures and canopies were so badly vandalised following the Reformation that soon after the Restoration the wall was boarded over and covered with a picture of the Last Judgement! In the roof gilded angels can be seen projecting from the 19c. hammer beams roof..

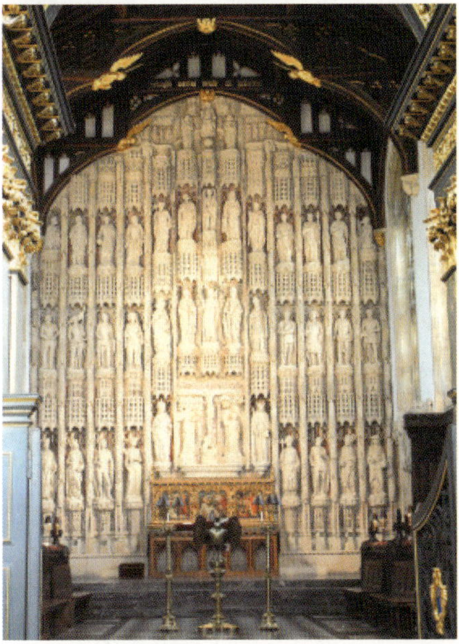

Brasses

Among the interesting monuments in the antechapel are several good small brasses, including a pair of half figures in ecclesiastical dress memorials to **David Lloyd and Thomas Baker †1510,** and a full-length figure of **Richard Spekynton †1490**. Although not accurate portraits, the faces are particularly beautiful.

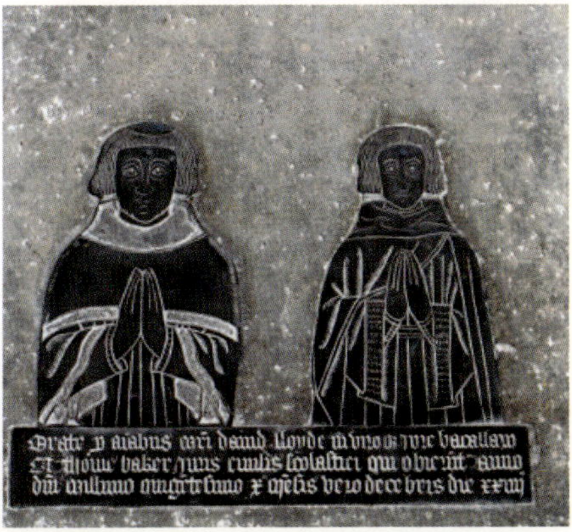

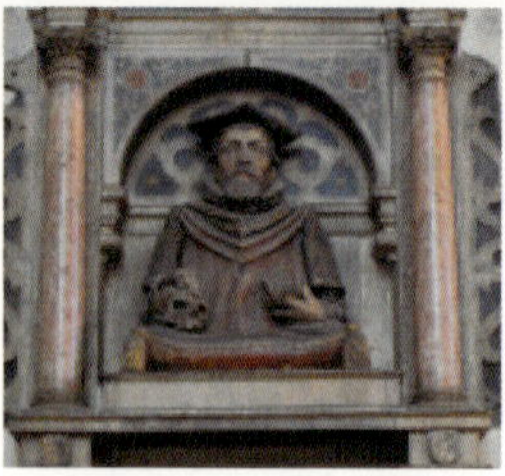

Robert Hovenden † 1614

Hovenden was a staunchly Protestant Warden, but he tried to save the sculpture of the reredos. His monument is similar to Robert Goodwin's in the cathedral: a coloured half figure with a book and skull in a Classical architectural surround. He was responsible for producing the first maps of the college's numerous properties.

Edward Man †1673
William Byrd

The oval cartouche above the entrance has a very rich (Pevsner calls it grisly) surround; a pair of horns of plenty discharging fruit, skulls, bones, coat of arms, surrounding a black marble inscription.

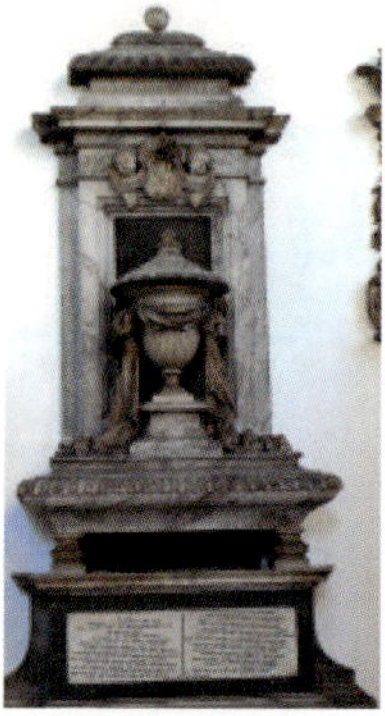

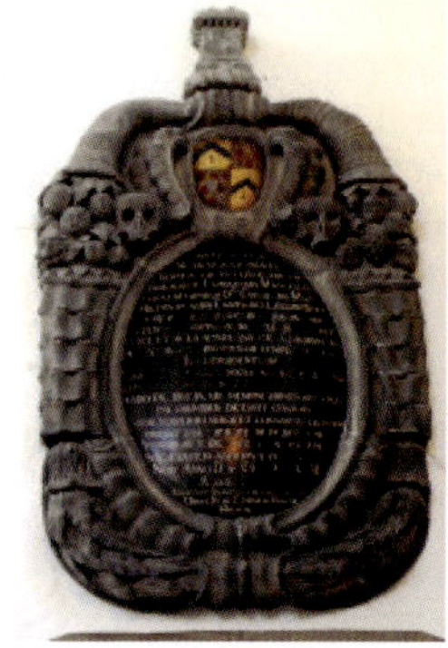

George Clarke †1736

Clark, a distinguished Renaissance man, lawyer, politician, amateur architect, and patron of Nicholas Hawksmoor, has a grand marble monument on the south wall. The sarcophagus with large urn and garlands is typical of baroque design of the early 18th century. A difficult college Fellow, because of a dispute with All Souls, Clark left his valuable collection of architectural drawings to Worcester College.

Corbels

Binoculars will reveal a fine array of corbels supporting the restored roof structure. As they were difficult to get at, many of them survived the destruction in the 16th and 17th-century.

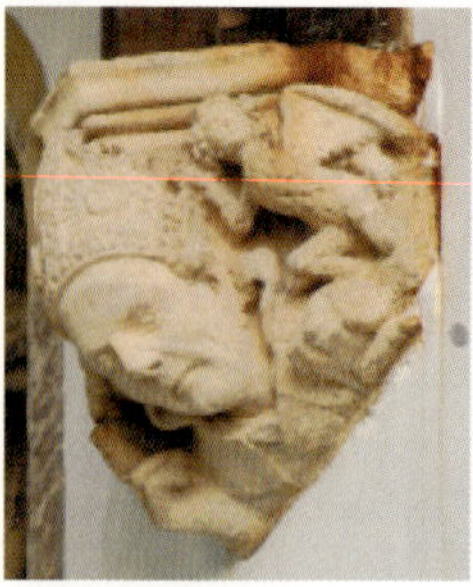

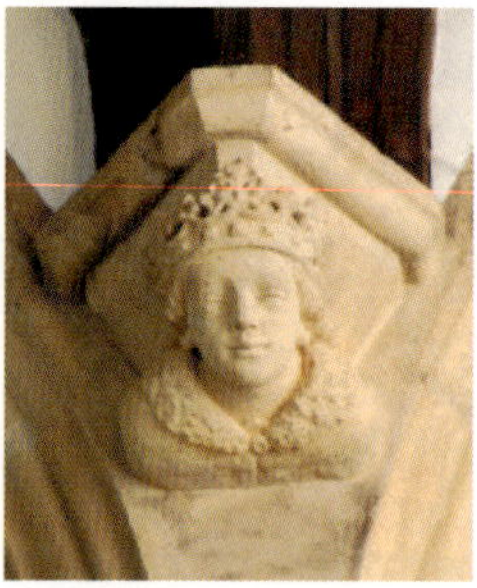

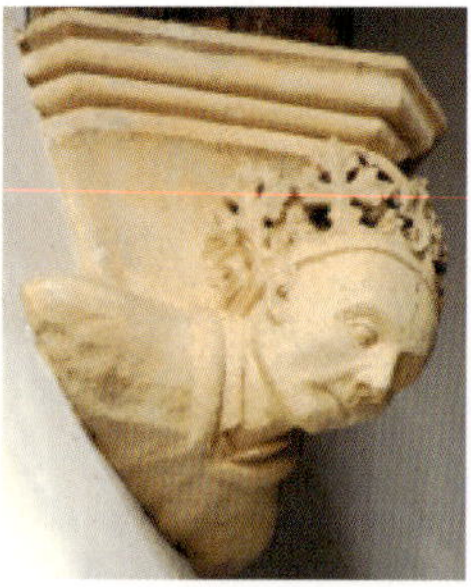

Grotesques

There are some amusing examples of grotesques above the windows of the front quad. Although modern they are in the sprit of the middle ages where some of the images are caricatures of college worthies. There is a large collection all over the city.

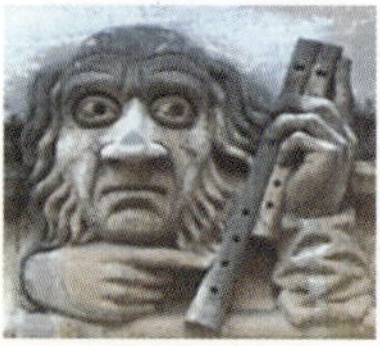

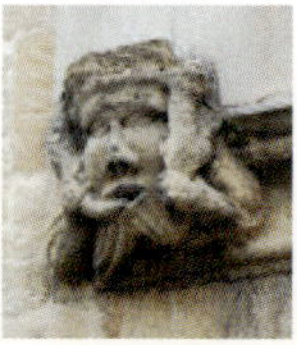

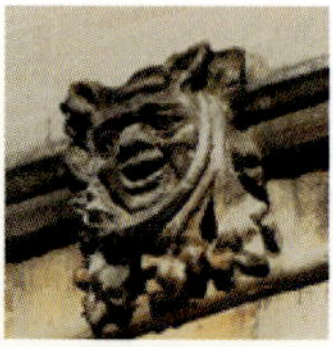

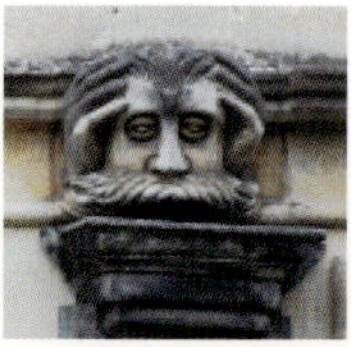

University College The College is not usually open to visitors. For permission Tel.01865 276602

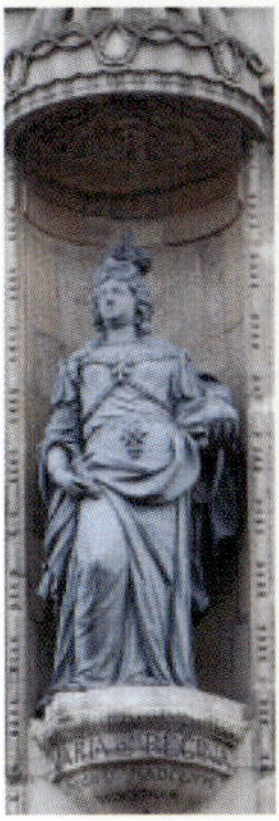

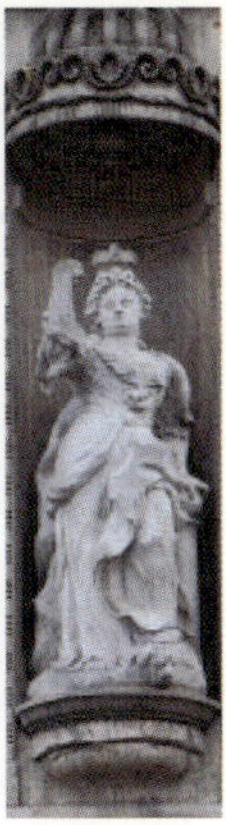

Like Merton, "Univ" (almost opposite All Souls) is a very early foundation, although none of the original buildings survive. Two Queens, **Anne** in a robust Baroque pose and a gentler **Mary II,** are in niches facing Queen Caroline across the High Street, while **James II** (of 1687) faces into the quad.

The Chapel

Sir William Jones † 1794.

This is one of several monuments in the antechapel by the distinguished sculptor John Flaxman, among the best pieces of their period in Oxford. Jones is shown in high relief writing the laws of India, for which he was responsible, watched by appreciative locals who stand beneath a collection of musical instruments. Flaxman, whose work was influenced by ancient Egyptian sculpture, also carved the **Chambers, Wetherell**, and **Rolleston** monuments here.

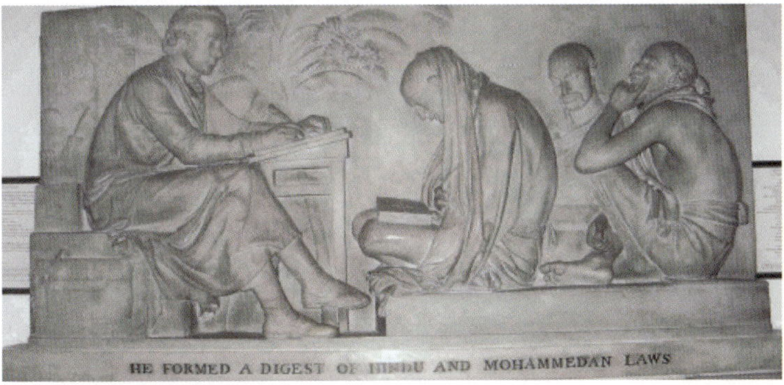

The Shelley Memorial

Many consider this the most famous of all the sculptural monuments in Oxford. The memorial is housed in its own domed building, facing the High Street. The gleaming white, naked body of **Shelley †1822** lies on top of a bronze base with the muse of Poetry and two winged lions. The poet is shown lying dead, as he did on the beach near La Spezia, Italy, where he drowned. The memorial, made by Onslow Ford in 1894, was probably too big (and erotic?) for the Protestant cemetery in Rome and was eventually given to the College, from which Shelley, as a rebellious student, had been expelled, without a degree, for circulating a political pamphlet.

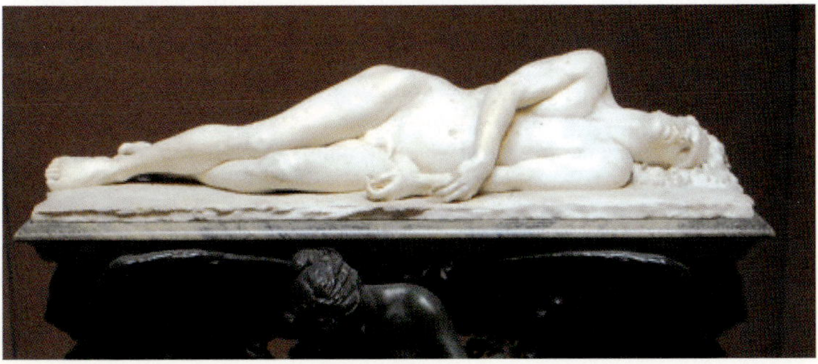

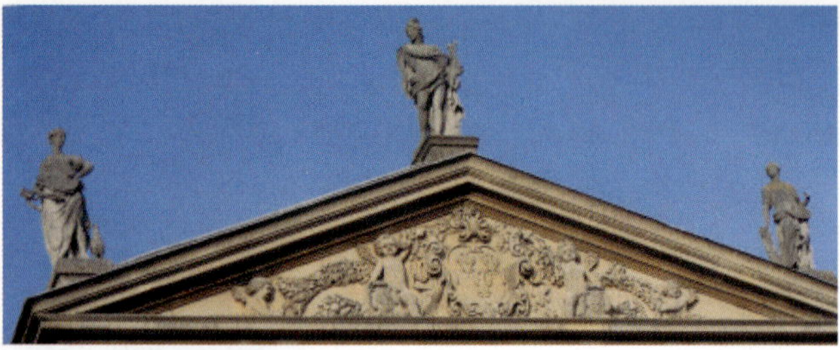

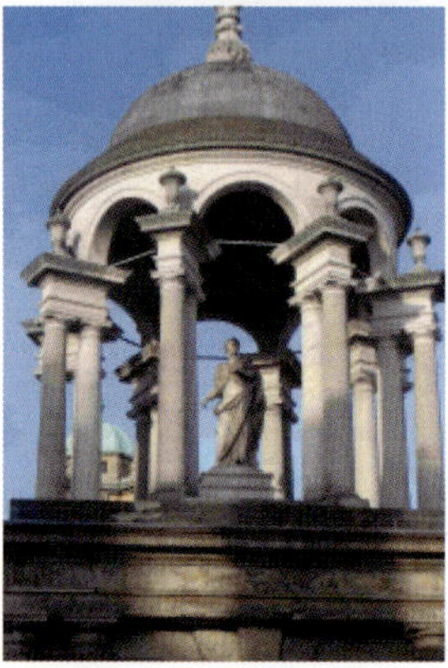

The Queen's College High Street

The College has one of the most impressive façades on the High Street, including the splendid temple-like rotunda above the entrance. This structure protects a full size figure of **Queen Caroline,** wife of George II, by *Henry Cheere,* one of the best early 18th-century sculptors. Cheere was also responsible for the figures on the pediment at the end of the eastern projecting range. (A similar, western group, was re-done in the 19th-century). Cheere's work was developing away from the Baroque into a lighter, more delicate style sometimes referred to as 'Rococo'.

Magdalen College Open generally 1pm-6pm but 12pm-6pm mid-July to early October. Fee charged.

Magdalen Tower marks the entrance to historic Oxford at the eastern end of the High Street. Turn right just inside the gatehouse, where there is a fine modern sculpture of Christ and Mary Magdalen (*David Wynne)* in Chaplain's Quad, a small courtyard recently and beautifully repaved and planted.

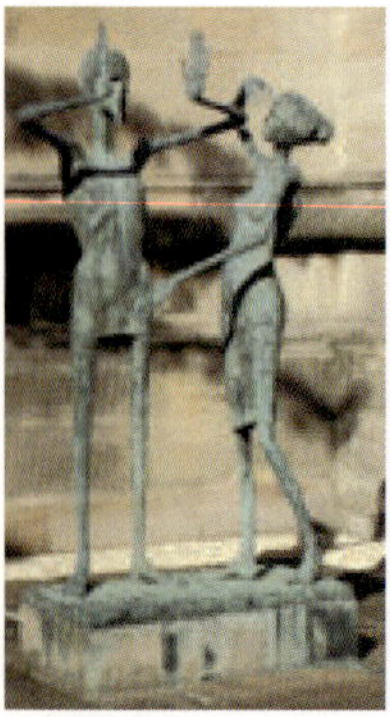

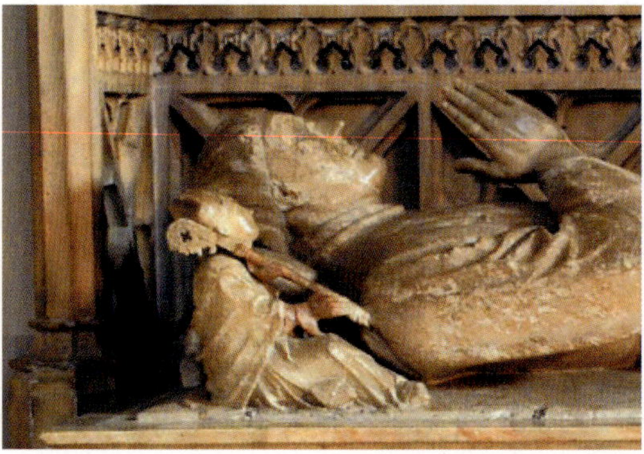

Chapel.

The Chapel was radically restored in the 19th century. Both the screen and the reredos at the east end are good reinstatements of 1829 by *Thomas Earp.*

The antechapel has several good memorials and misericords including:

Richard Patten (†1450) East Wall

The best sculpture at Magdalen is, appropriately, a full-length effigy of the father of the Founder, brought here in the 19th century. It lies in a recess and has miniature figures of the Founder, Bishop Waynflete, and his brother, on either side of the head.

John and Thomas Lyttleton †1635 East Wall *Nicholas Stone*
Above the Patten tomb there is a touching memorial to two brothers who died attempting to rescue each other.

William Langton †1626 North Wall
Below the copy of *Leonardo da Vinci's* "Last Supper", this is a slightly earlier and very different memorial, showing Langton, reading a book, seated below a skull. The surroundings are very elaborate, with a Renaissance entablature and two female figures holding open the drapery.

Laurence Humphry †1590 South Wall
This is an early example of a half-figure scholar memorial, including symbols representing the deceased's life. Humphry, a virulent anti-Catholic who campaigned against the use of vestments, is apparently preaching. His 'pulpit' still has Gothic details

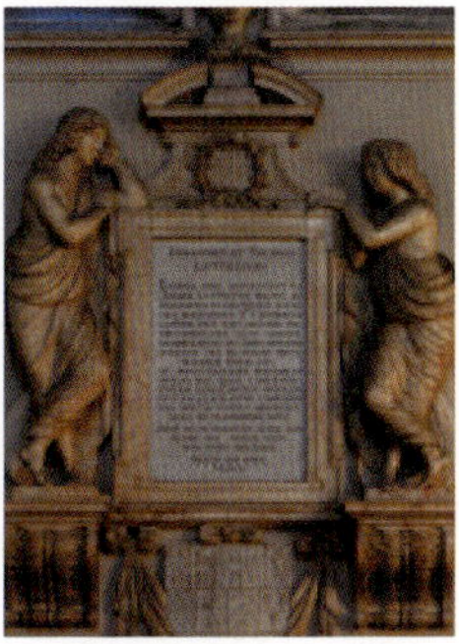

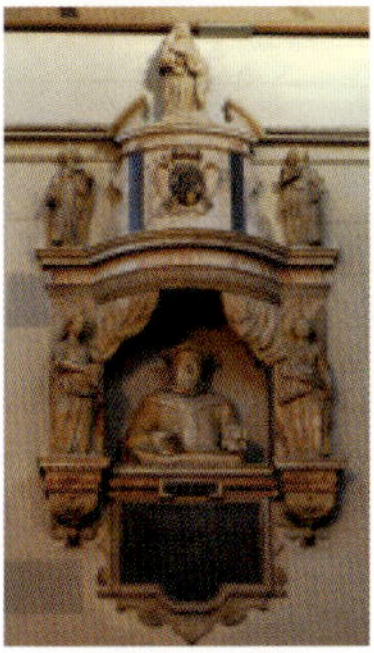

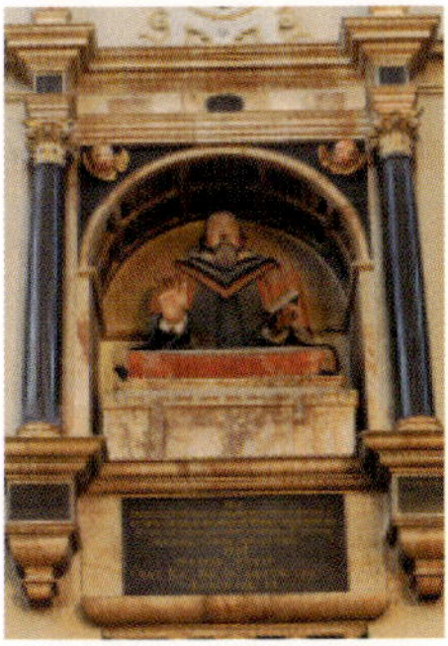

Misericords
At Magdalen there is a rare opportunity in Oxford for visitors to study misericords at close range. The carvings are under the stalls, removed from the chapel in the 19th- century and now along the walls of the antechapel. Subjects include a monkey, an owl, a fox and geese, a horse on its back, and a pair of wrestlers.

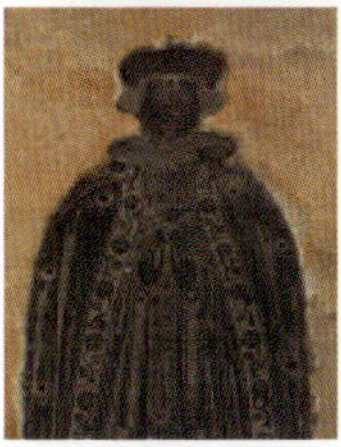

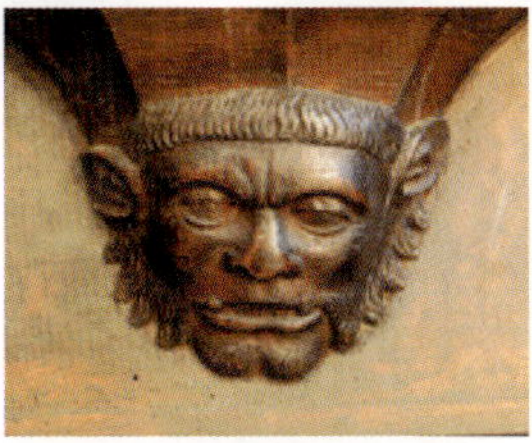

Brasses
Although the Magdalen brasses are not spectacular, like the misericords they are easy to study. Some are now mounted on the wall.

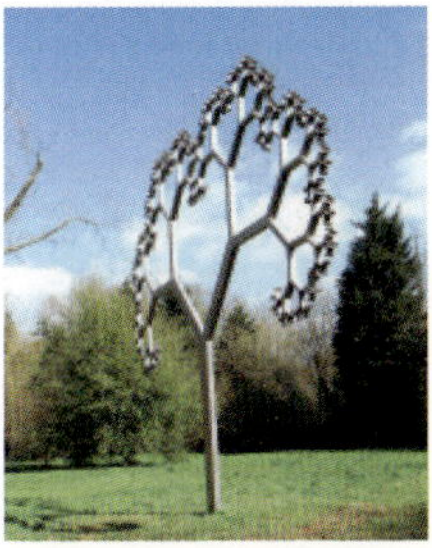

The Y Bat 2008, Willow Meadow by *Mark Wallinger*
The recent and the biggest piece of sculpture in Oxford, commissioned to mark the 550th anniversary of the College's foundation, is beyond the bridge at the far end of the long and delightful "Addison's Walk". The sculpture was inspired by ancient college trees, the antlers of the college deer, and Gothic tracery. The structure is almost hidden amongst the foliage.

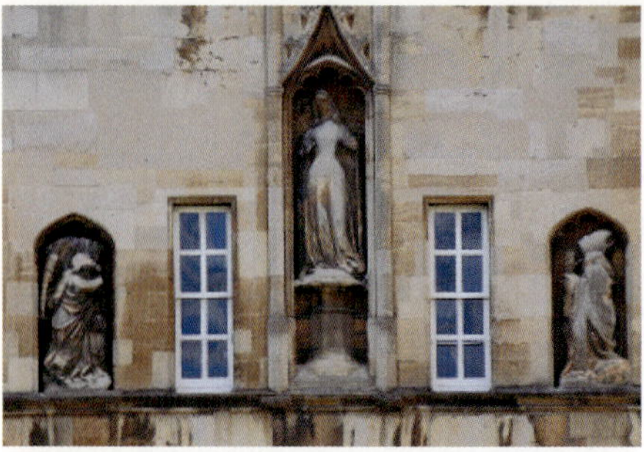

New College

The New College Lane gate is generally open from 11am -5pm Easter to October. Fee charged. October-Easter entry through the Holywell Street Gate 2pm-4pm.

The college was founded in 1379 by William of Wykeham and became the model for future Oxford foundations. Wykeham's figure, kneeling, together with that of angels and the Virgin, is shown on both sides of the gate tower. In the passage leading to the Cloister there is a small bronze figure of a man fighting against a storm, by Max Sokol. The large gaunt figures spaced around the Cloister were removed in the 19th century from the spire of the Church of St Mary the Virgin in the High Street.

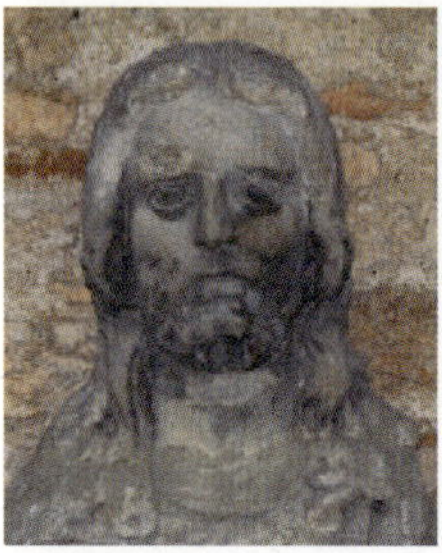

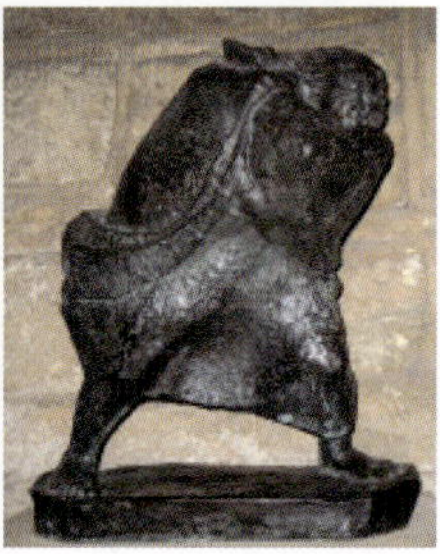

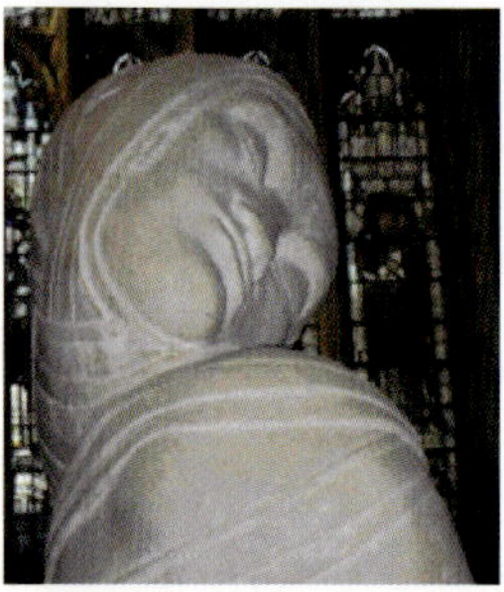

Chapel

The most striking feature of this magnificent interior is the statue of **Lazurus,** *Jacob Epstein* (1951) in the antechapel.The figure's twisted form, struggling like an emerging butterfly from the constraints of his burial bandages, stands under the incongruous, painted glass of the west window (after *Reynolds)*. This is the most important modern sculpture in Oxford and an important piece of 20th-century British art.

Scholar Memorials Antechapel

The best memorial, **Hugh Barker † 1632,** by *Nicholas Stone*, shows the distinguished lawyer as a half figure looking splendid in a magnificent ruff. **Robert Pike †1647,** also a half-figure in a black marble recess, is much more contemplative. Both are on the west wall. Opposite, another half figure of **Michel Woodward †1675,** is less life-like. In contrast, the memorial to **Charles Burlton †1836,** by *Humphrey Hopper* (North wall), has a graceful female, prostrate on the ground. (see page 25)

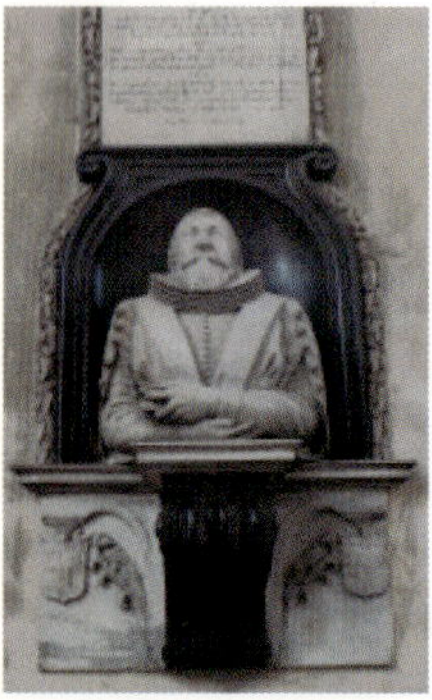

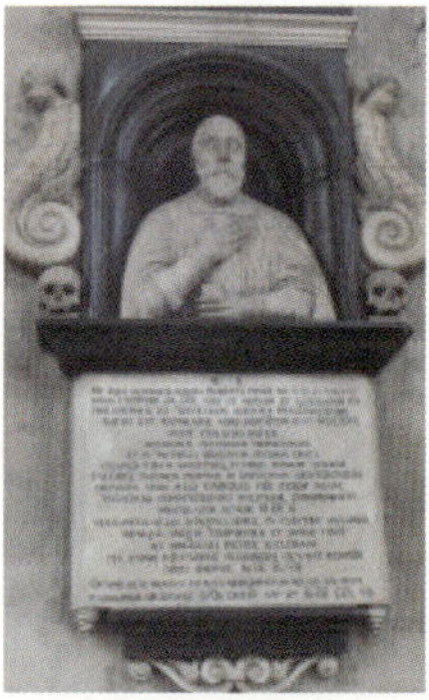

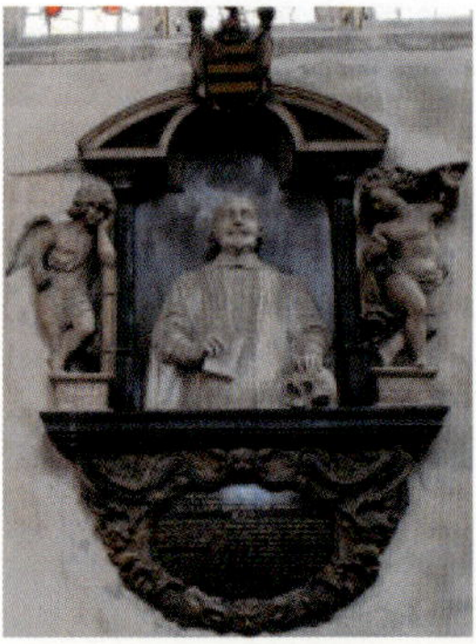

On the south wall a huge plaque lists the young men of New College killed fighting for Britain during the First World War. To the left, a smaller plaque list young Germans, former members of New College, who died fighting against them! The carved letters are excellent examples of the work of the sculptor Eric Gill.

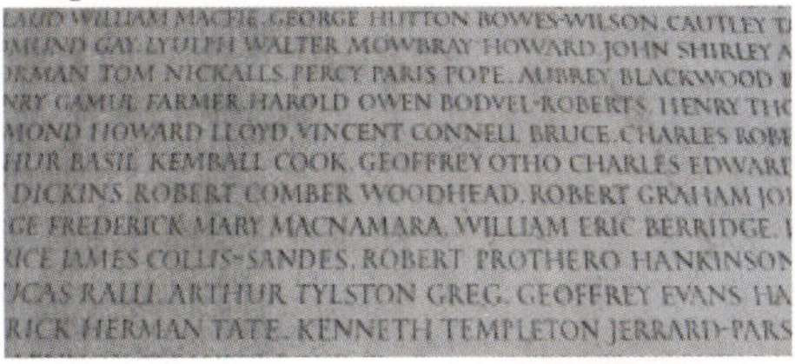

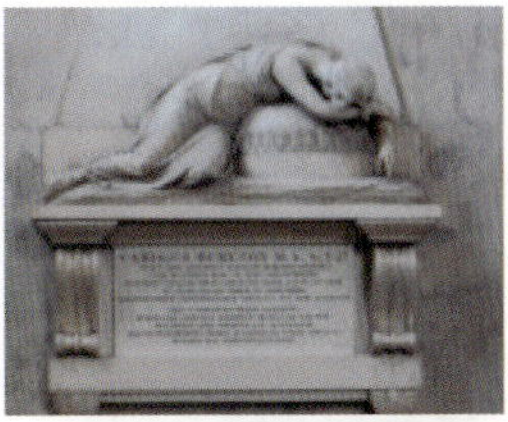

Misericords

Under the stalls in the chapel there are some of the best 14th-century misericords in Oxford. Those at the end of the passages between the stalls can usually be seen if the seats are lifted. Each ledge, carved out of a single piece of oak, has a carefully balanced design. The scenes are full of detail, animation and expression. Some of the figures are naturalistic shown doing everyday activities, while others are mythical or grotesque. Between the stalls there are lovely carved elbow-rests.

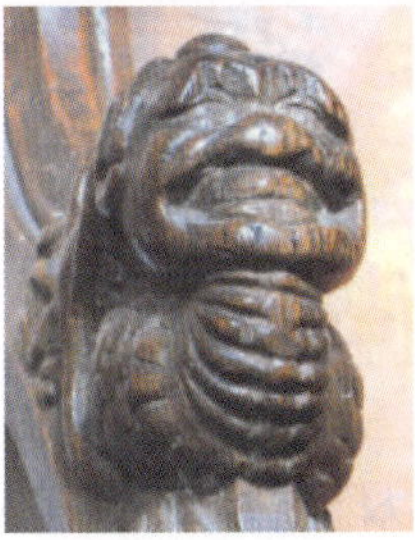

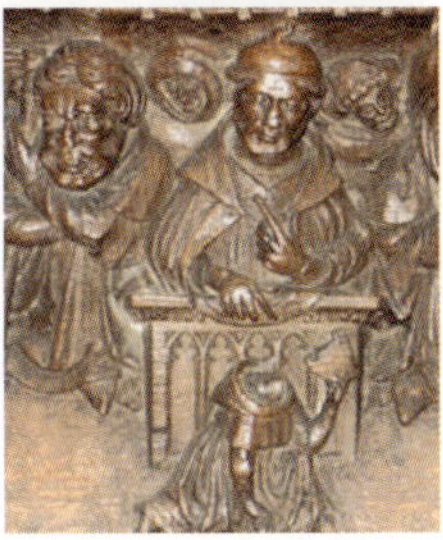

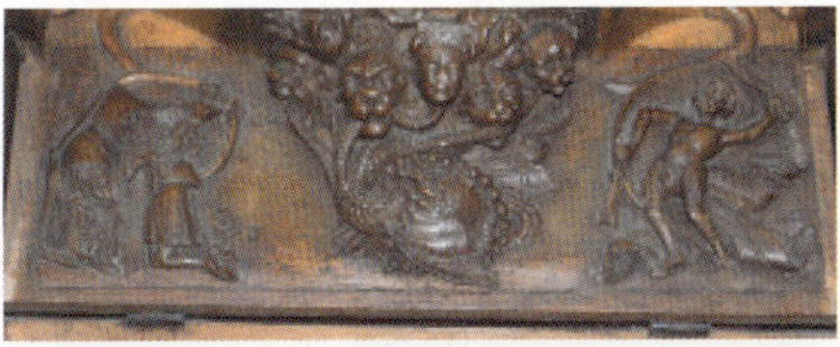

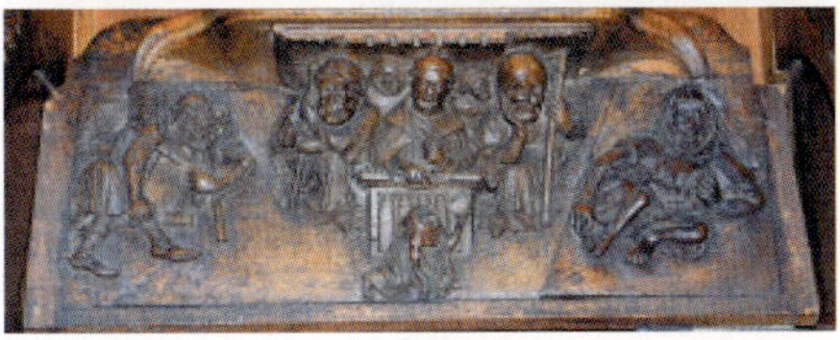

Reredos

The medieval display which filled the east wall of the chapel was destroyed by the Puritans. It must have been splendid. The present one, a good Victorian reproduction, creates a wonderful impression. The spectacular cantilevered gilded angels on the hammer beam roof are also Victorian.

Brasses Antechapel North Transept.

Most of the large collection of 15th-century brasses, protected by a barrier, are hard to view. They include a fine large example to **Thomas Cranley †1417,** with his mitre and cross staff, under a triple canopy with crockets and pinnacles.

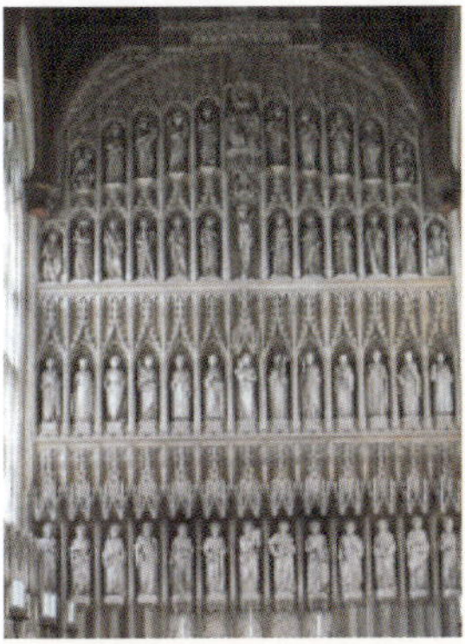

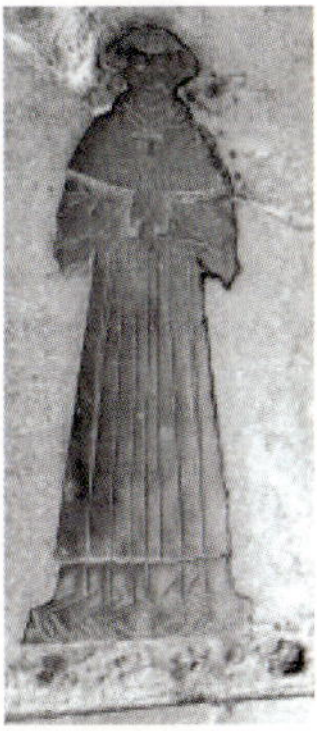

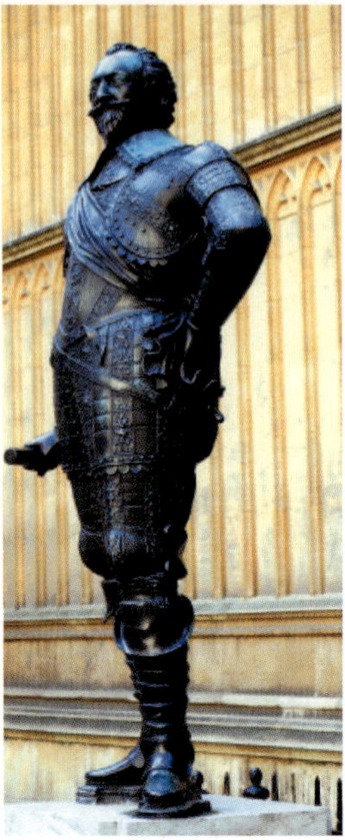

The University of Oxford

The School's Quadrangle

Earl of Pembroke *Hubert Le Sueur*

The statue of Pembroke, the Chancellor of the University, stands majestically in splendid court armour and boots before the door to the Divinity School. The figure is based on a portrait by Rubens. It was cast early in the 17th century and placed here in 1722. It is the best example of bronze sculpture in Oxford.

This very accomplished piece contrasts with the much cruder stone figure of **King James I** (by *John Clarke*, but restored) on the richly-carved entrance tower of the Classical Orders c.1620. The King is seated under a canopy, in a niche flanked by the winged figure of Fame and a kneeling figure representing the University. The figure of the King was originally painted in vivid colours, which apparently embarrassed his majesty when he visited Oxford to take part in a learned disputation, a popular intellectual entertainment at the time.

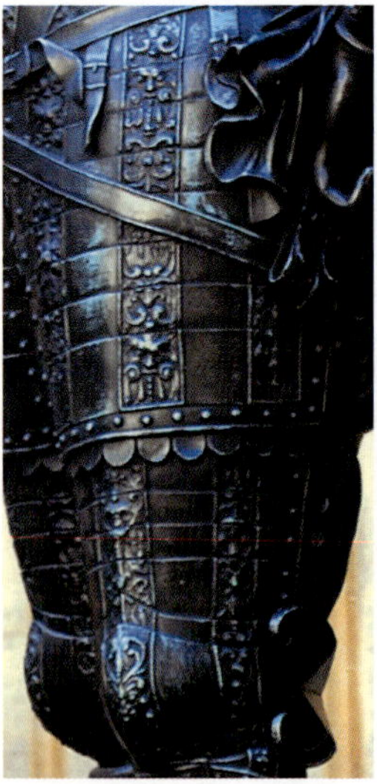

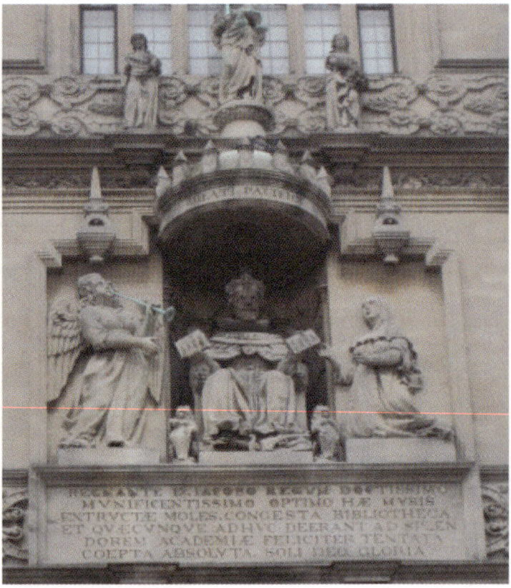

The Divinity School West End of the Bodleian Quadrangle. Fee charged.

This, the first lecture room built specifically for the University, started in 1420 and finished 60 years later by master mason *William Orchard* (see also the Cathedral Choir). The marvellous vaulted ceiling makes this the finest university building anywhere. At the junctions of the vaulting ribs there are 455 sculptured bosses, mainly coats of arms and initials of donors (and several of Orchard himself), but including a Virgin and Child and animal and human figures. Dropping from the main ribs, miniature pendants contain holy figures. On both of the end walls there are figures of bishops, monks, angels, and seraphims, arranged below a Madonna and Child. Many carvers must have been employed in the creation, probably under the direction of *John Maisingham.*

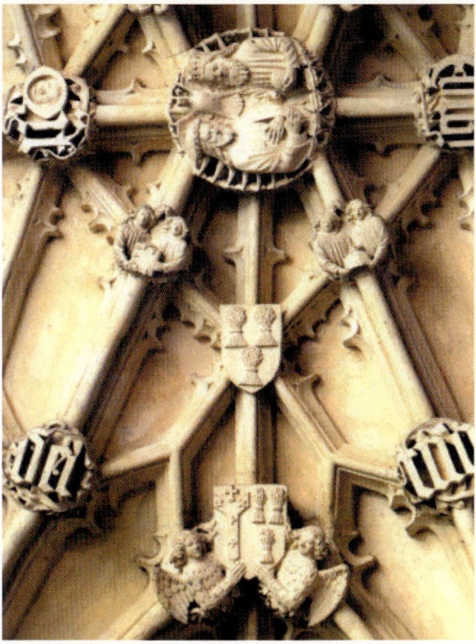

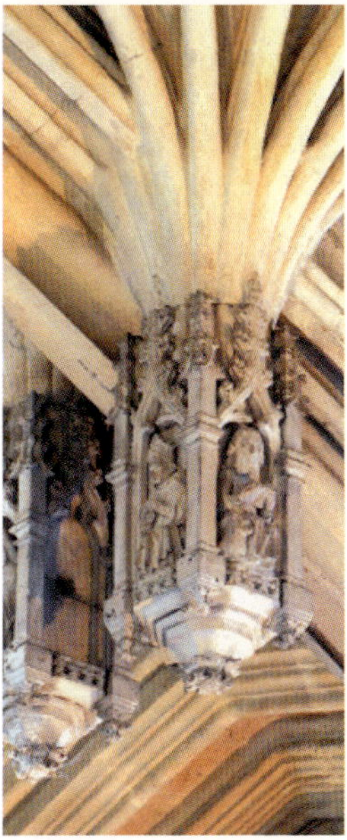

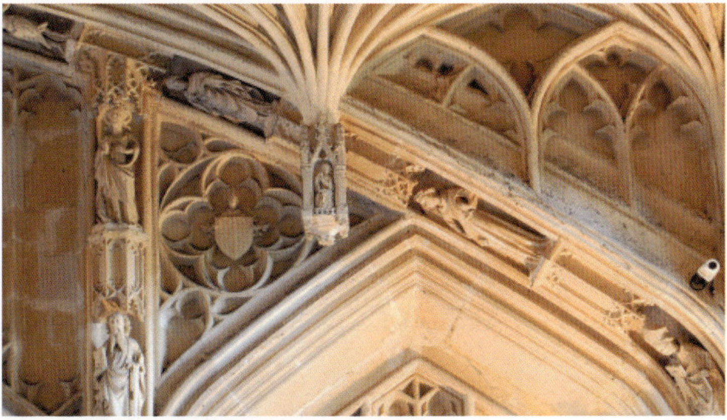

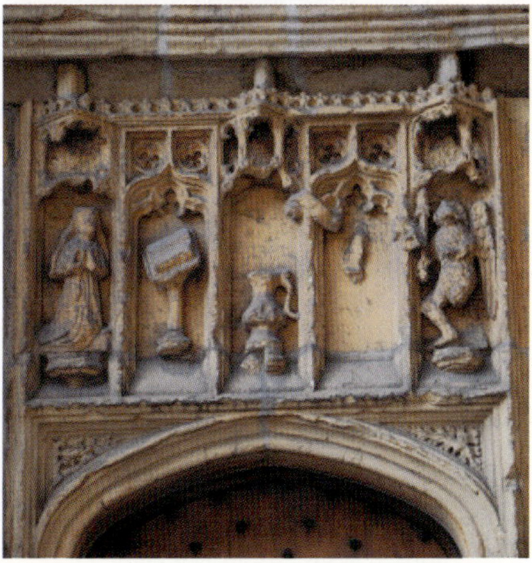

Hertford College

There is a remarkable survivor from the Middle Ages, almost hidden on a wall to the left of the gate opposite the eastern façade of the Clarendon building. The small panel decorated a chapel which stood alongside a gate in the city wall. It shows the Virgin Mary, visited by the Angel Gabriel. When the panel was cleaned recently all traces of the original colour had disappeared. It is a lovely remnant of a vanished age.

Broad Street

The Clarendon Building

North of the Schools Quadrangle

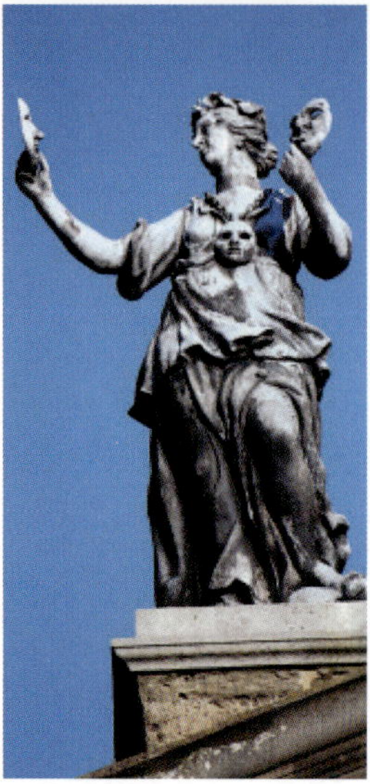

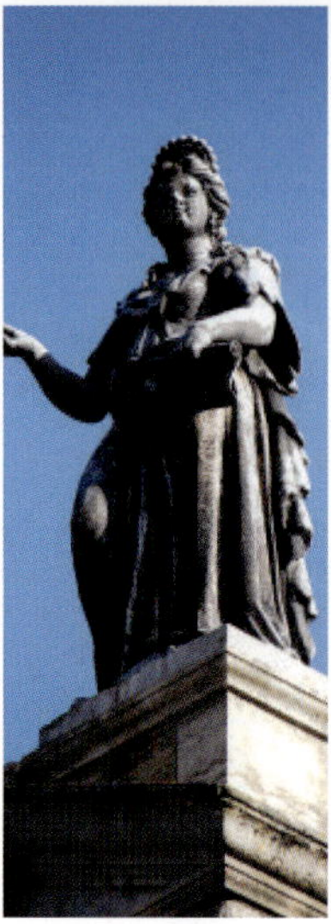

Nine full-size figures decorate the roof of this muscular building by *Nicholas Hawksmoor.* These figures, representing the muse goddesses of the arts, were designed by *Sir James Thornhill* and cast in lead by *Francis Bird* in 1721. There are two recent replacements in fibre-glass indistinguish-able from the rest. On the west wall there is another figure of the Earl of Clarendon (also by *Francis Bird).*

Sheldonian Screen 'The Boundary of Terms'

The huge hairy heads, philosophers (or emperors), which top the pillars of the screen to the area in front of the Sheldonian Theatre were commissioned by Christopher Wren in 1669. The originals were carved by *William Byrd* but were replaced in the 19th century, and once again in 1970 by *Michael Black.* Although controversial at the time, the new heads are now an accepted (and much photographed) oddity of the Oxford scene.

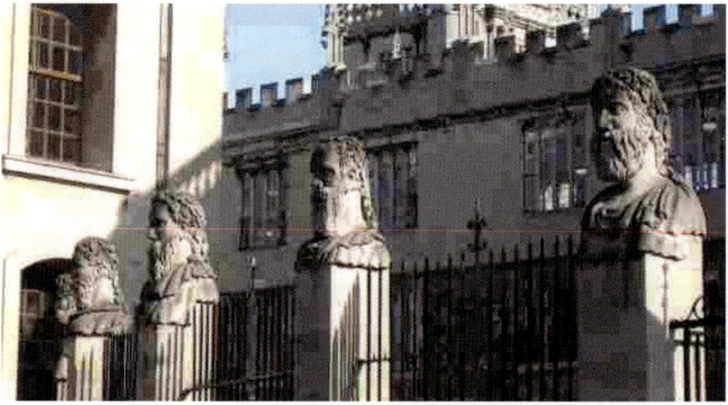

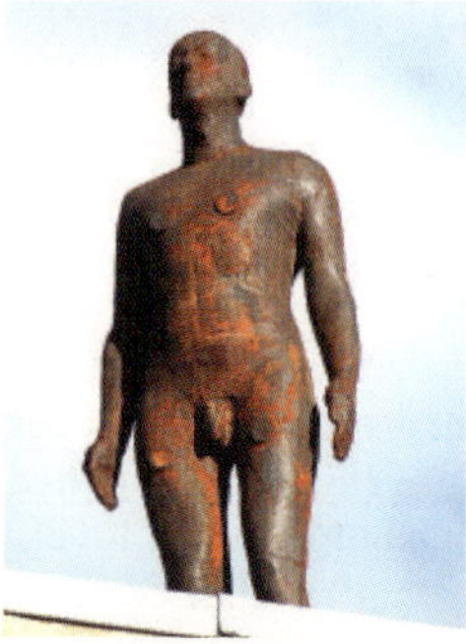

Exeter College / Blackwells Art Book Shop

Looking down from the corner of Broad Street and the Turl the most a recent addition to public sculpture is a life size figure of sculptor *Anthony Gormley* (2009). It is one of many castings of the artist's body which can be seen in other parts of the country including a crowd of them on the beach near Liverpool. Gormley's huge "Angel of the North" alongside the M1 is the best known and best loved modern sculpture in England.

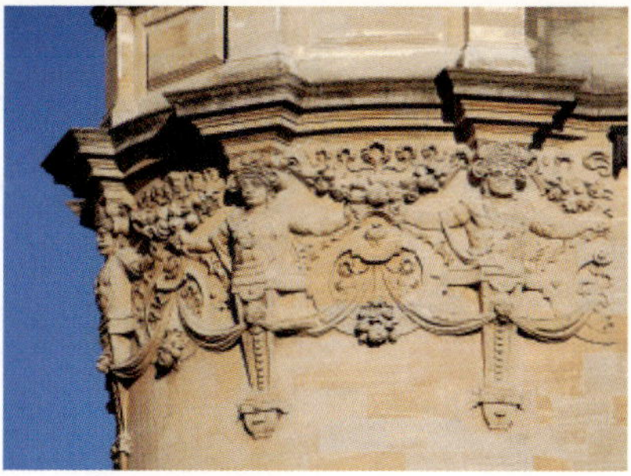

Indian Institute

The corner of this witty, late 19th-century building (by *Basil Champneys*) at the end of Broad Street, has a ring of oriental gods holding hands, at high level, and lower down, some attractive elephant heads. They are the work of the sculptor *Aumonier.*

Trinity College

Usually open during the afternoon. Fee charged.

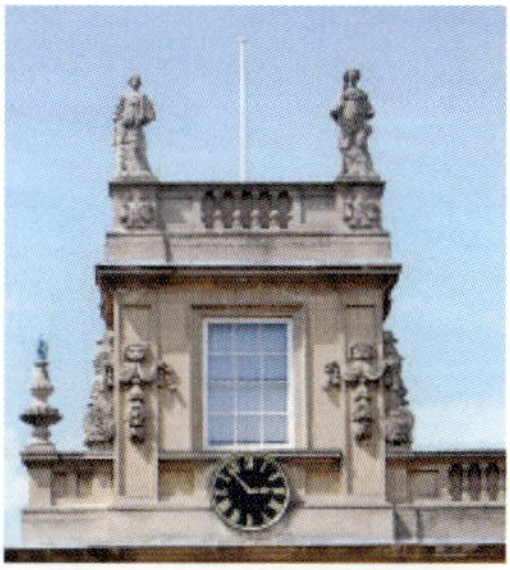

The college was founded in 1555, on the site of an earlier monastic one closed by Henry VIII. There are four badly weathered statues, Geometry, Astronomy, Theology, and Medicine, on top of the gate tower, which may have been designed by Christopher Wren.

The Chapel

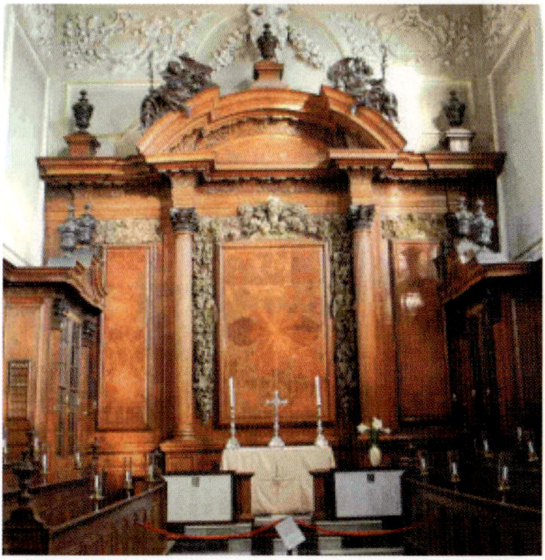

Entered from Durham quad beyond the gate tower, the chapel is the chief glory of Trinity with one of the best late 17th-century interiors in England. The entrance screen, the plaster ceiling, the walls, and above all the reredos, are unified by a single design idiom. Even the Founder's Elizabethan monument has been concealed in a glass-fronted cupboard to the left of the altar to avoid spoiling the ensemble.

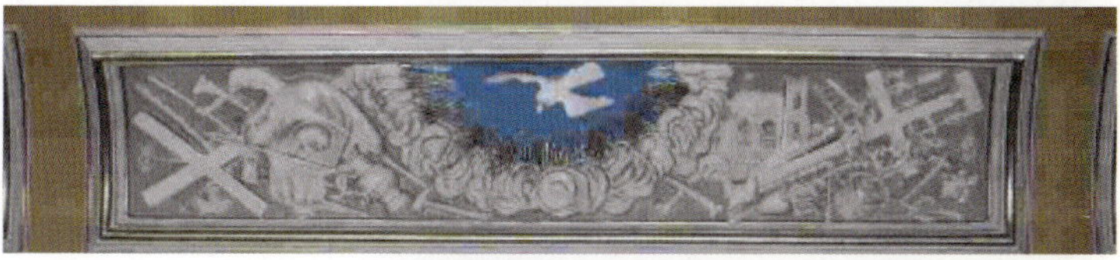

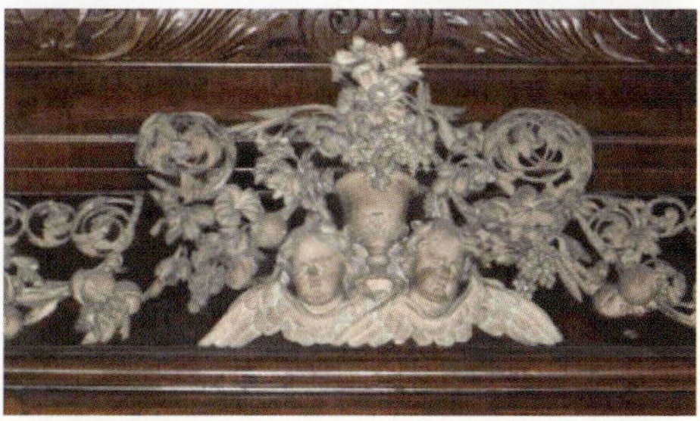

Walls are panelled in juniper wood, the carvings are in lime. Most authorities agree that some of the carvings are by Grinling Gibbons, the most famous of all English wood-carvers. Gibbons was certainly working at this time at nearby Blenheim Palace.

On both the screen and the reredos above the altar graceful female figures sit slightly precariously on top of a typical late Baroque broken pediment. Framing the plain panelling there are beautifully delicate representations of fruit and foliage, with cherubic faces peeping out here and there; withal, a joyful feast to be savoured slowly.

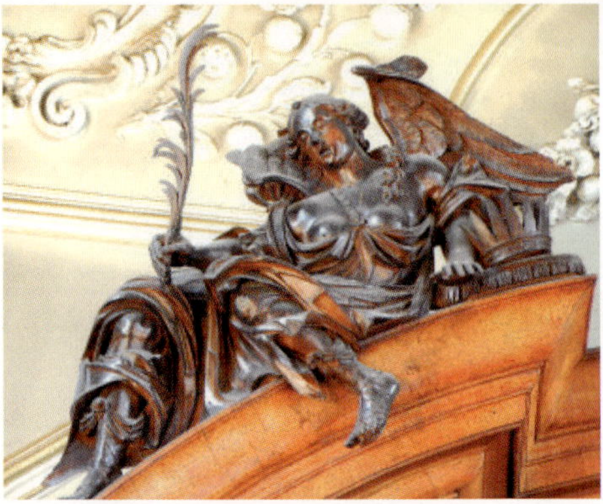

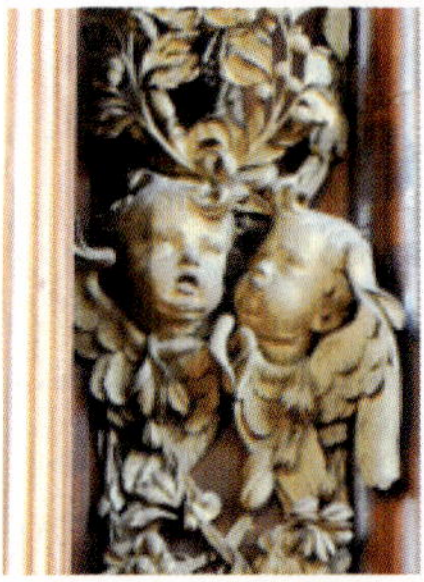

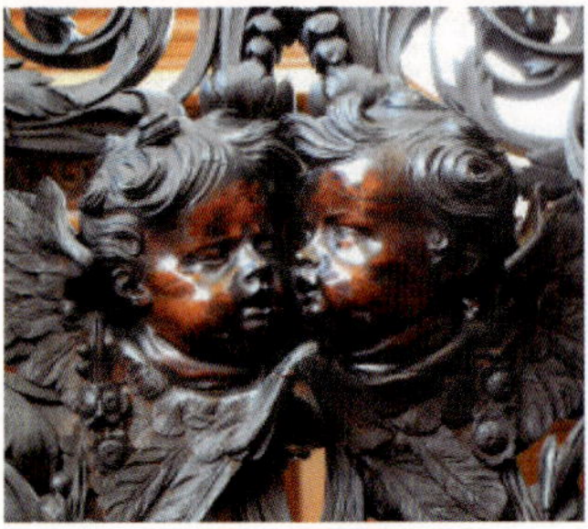

Wadham College

The college is usually open in the afternoon.

A statue of James I, a little stiff but more flattering than that in the Bodleian Quadrangle, stands in the middle, above those of the Founders, Dorothy and (in court armour) Nicholas Wadham, on the tower of the orders (c.1613) opposite the entrance. All three figures are restorations.

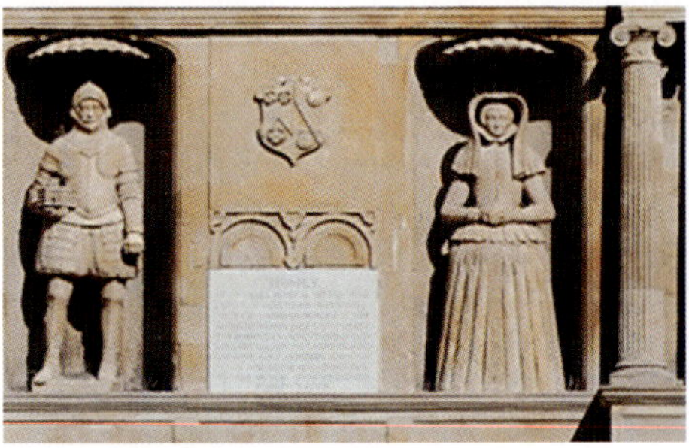

The chapel

There are many memorial tablets in the antechapel, including those of **John French †1688,** a cartouche with garlands and dolphins, and **John Upton †1686,** with two cherubs (or putti) and drapery. More unusual is the lead profile of **Thomas Joy,** killed in Iraq in 1915.

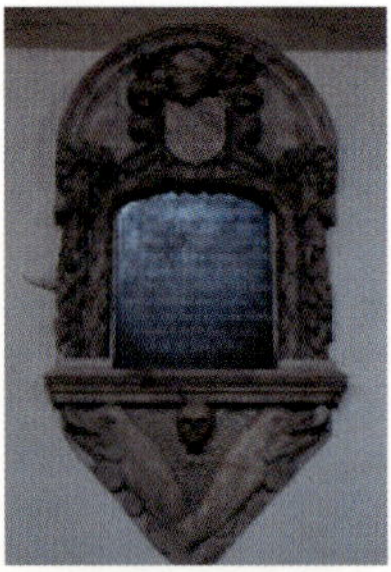

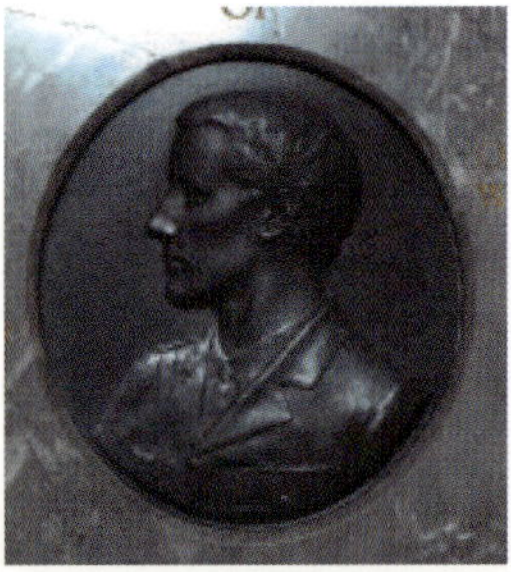

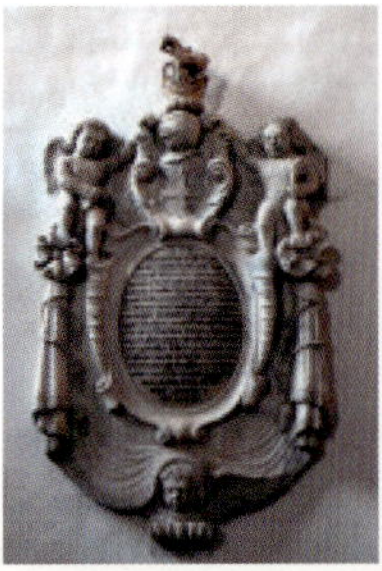

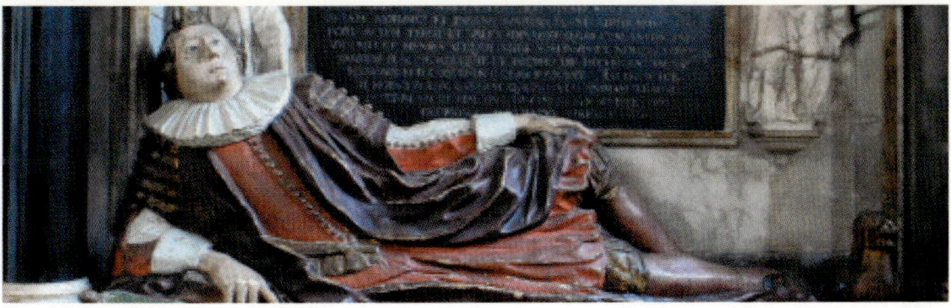

Sir John Portman †1642

On one of the most elaborate and colourful memorials in Oxford, a youthful figure reclines in a relaxed pose, looking heavenwards. He is housed in a splendid Renaissance structure with several female mourners, putti, a shield of arms, and old Father Time, complete with a large scythe, on the top.

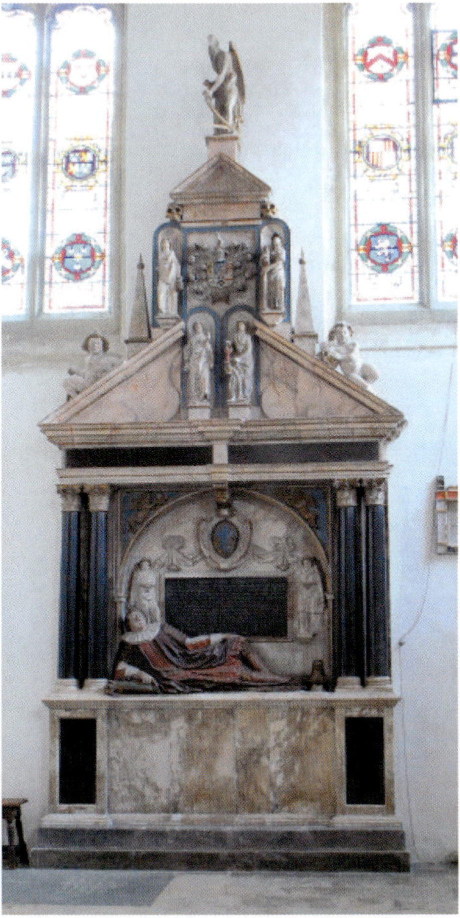

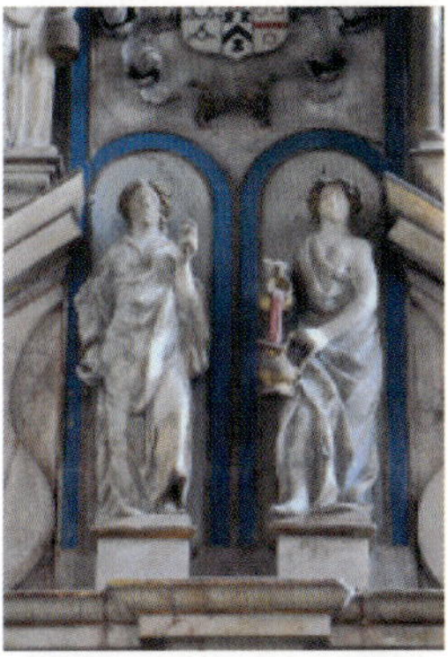

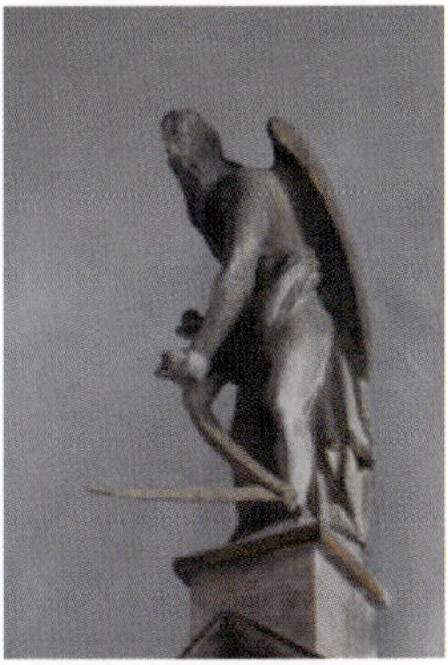

Fellows Garden (At the eastern end of the chapel)

There is a remarkable sculpture here by *John Doubleday* of the redoubtable Warden **Maurice Bowra †1971,** ("the greatest don of his era"), whose half figure is seen seated on a chair, a joke which echoes many 17th-century scholar monuments. It would have amused the celebrated, eccentric Warden.

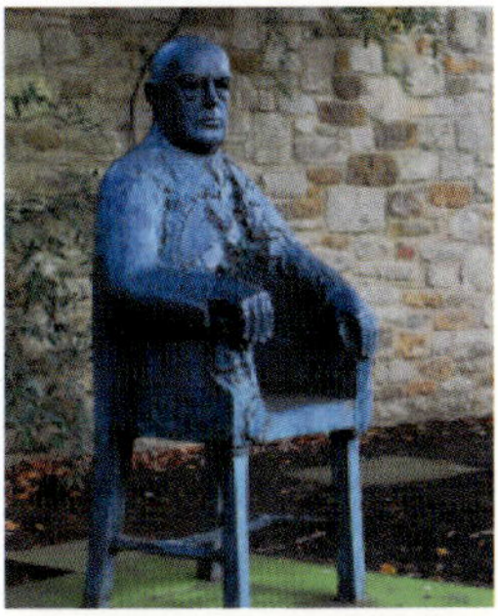

University Museum of Natural History

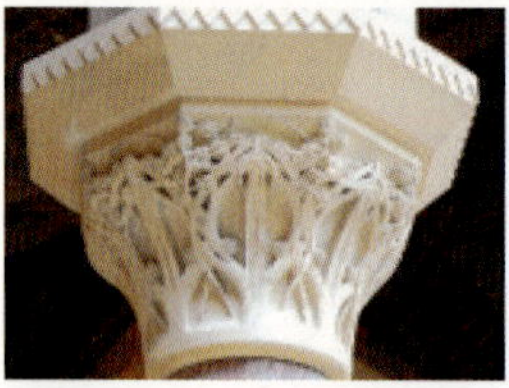
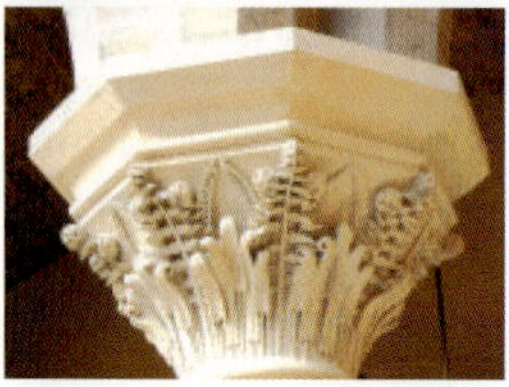
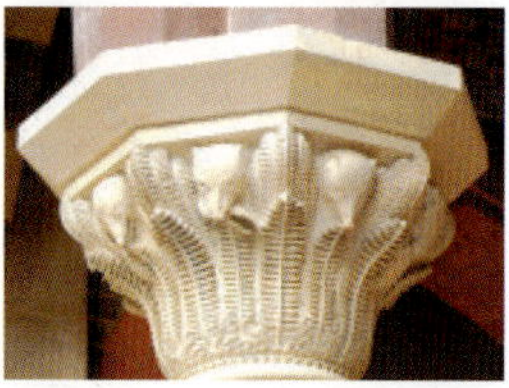
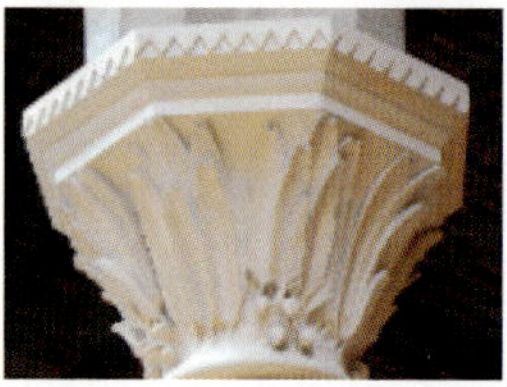

The museum is usually open from 10am to 5pm.

Everyone living in Oxford, and every tourist, should visit the University Museum, a fine piece of Victorian architecture, with fascinating, attractively exhibited collections of Natural History and one of the best places to see samples of excellent Victorian sculpture.

The most interesting work was done by members of the red-bearded, eccentric, O'Shea family, illustrating John Ruskin's theory of the creative talent of workman. The O'Sheas were employed to carve many of the details outside and inside of the building, most notably some of the capitals of the columns around the arcade on the west side (the rest are later). Each capital is an exquisite work of art, a stylized depiction of a plant form which they had studied in the Botanic Gardens. Some of the designs anticipate the work of Art Nouveau artists 50 years later. The delightful animals on the capitals flanking the entrance in the porch were probably also by this family. Their decoration of the windows on the façade of the building remains unfinished. The O'Sheas were thrown off the job for some disrespectful caricatures of the senior staff of the museum, and for spending too long at lunch, drinking Guinness. Either way, it was a great loss.

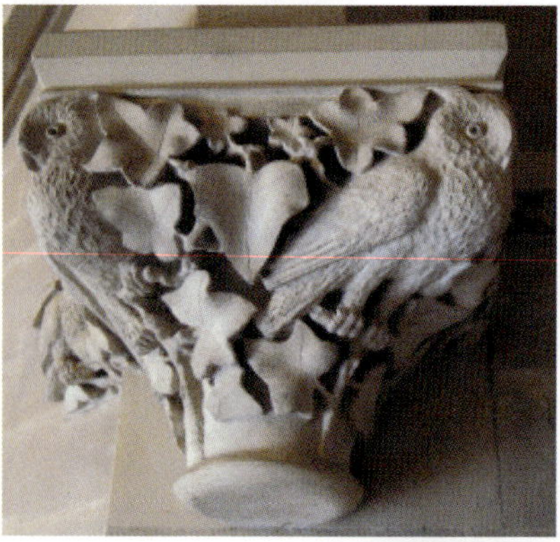
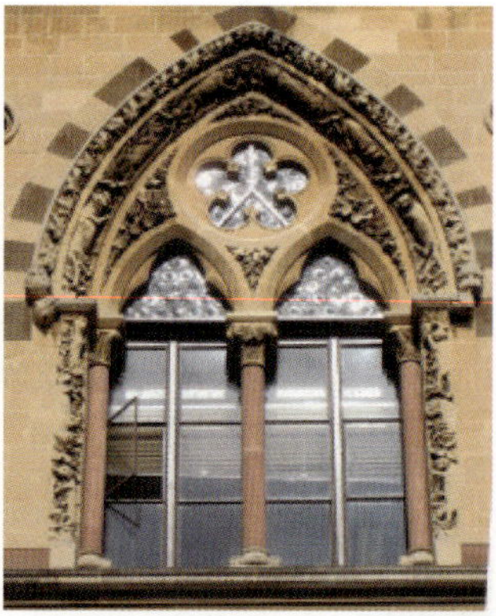

Every opportunity to employ individual craftsmen was taken. Even the mass-produced cast iron columns have capitals which are excellent examples of wrought-iron decorative craft which we have not seen before in Oxford. Like everything in the museum, it is based on natural forms.

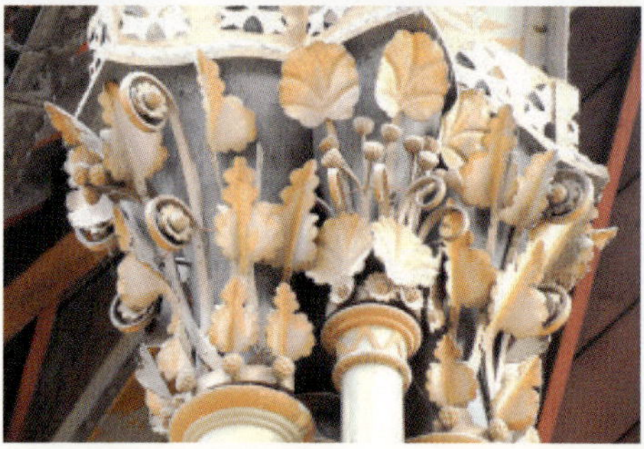

Each pillar supporting the gallery was to have a life-size figure of a famous scientist in front of it. These sculptures were to be paid for by subscription. Only 19 were forthcoming. The donors commissioned some of the best available Victorian sculptors. **Charles Darwin (2)** and **Roger Bacon (3)** by *Henry Hope Pinker,* and **William Harvey (4)** *by Henry Weekes*. In addition to the full-size figures there are several good portrait busts. See especially the bust of the architect of the building, **Benjamin Woodward (1)** *by Alexander Munro*, who died tragically young. Don't fail to also visit the Pitt Rivers Museum where there is a feast of ethnic sculpture.

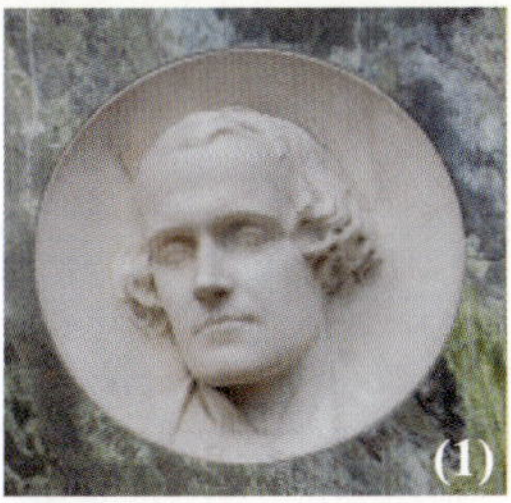
(1)

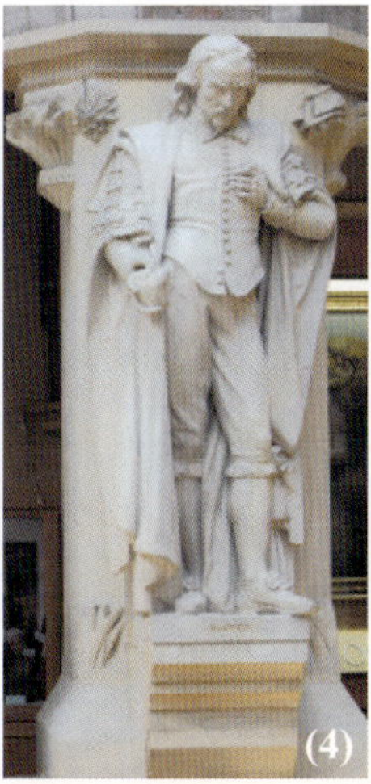
(4)

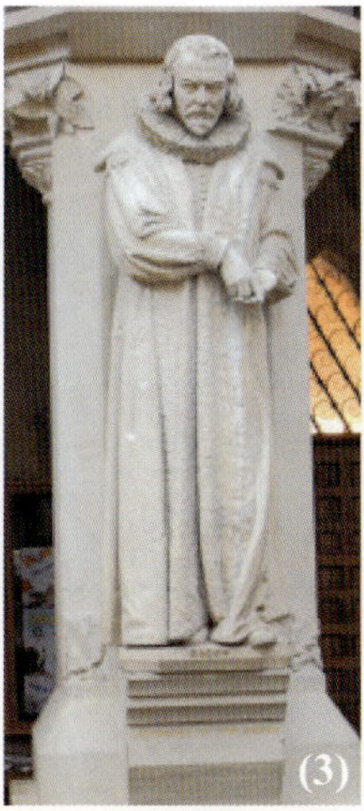
(3)

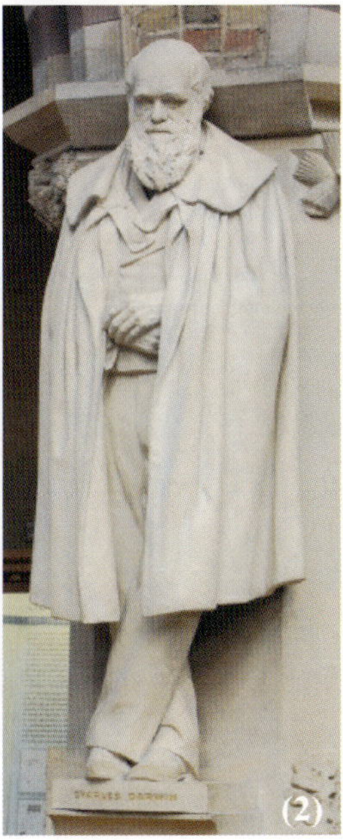
(2)

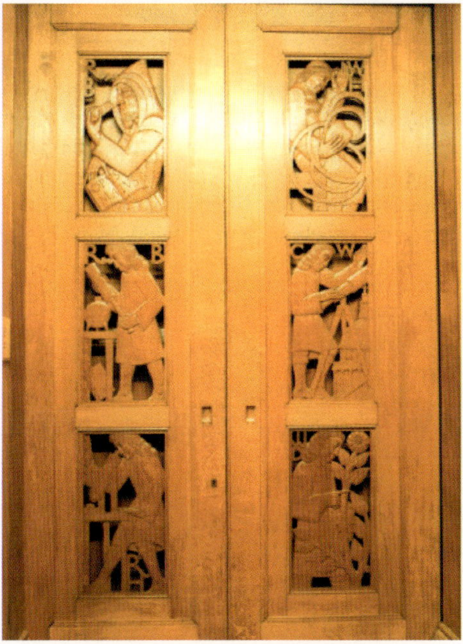

Radcliffe Science Library

People with a Bodleian ticket (or with special permission) should not miss the chance to see a pair of carved wooden doors on the first floor, by *Eric Gill* (1936). Each of the six panels has stylised portraits of Oxford's best-known scientists, together with their initials and symbols of the achievements. This is an interesting example of the work of one of the best sculptors of the 20th century. (See his work at St John's, at New College, and at St Alban's Church.)

St John's College

Usually open 1pm-5pm

St John's, on the eastern side of St Giles, took over the buildings of St Bernard's College after the Reformation. The original statue of St Bernard is on the outside of the gate tower. A modern figure of St John, by Eric Gill, is high up on the inside, facing Front Quad

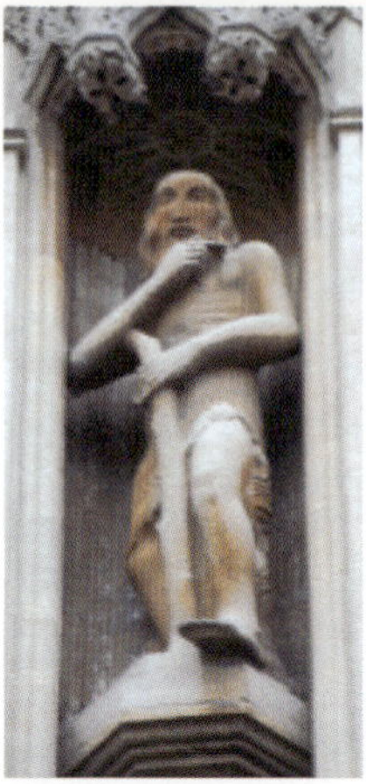

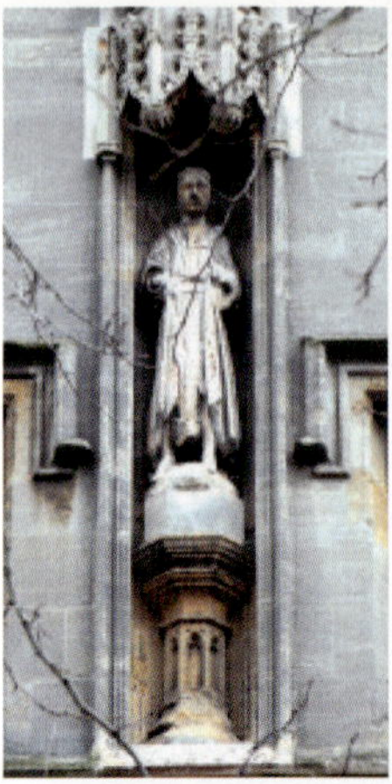

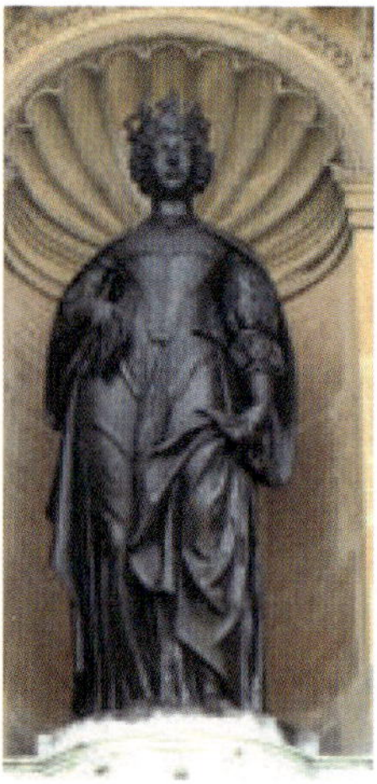

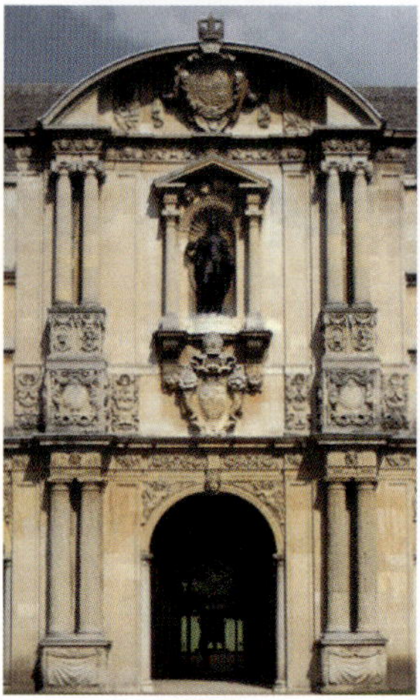

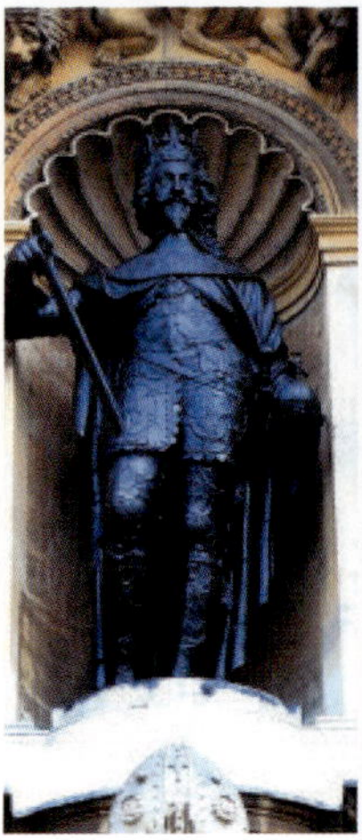

Canterbury Quadrangle.

This quad, certainly the most sumptuous in the University, has two magnificently carved Renaissance portals (built 1636) opposite each other, framing life-size bronze statues of **King Charles I** and his queen **Henrietta Maria,** both by *Le Sueur*. In the spandrels between the columns there are roundels with busts of the Virtues and Arts, by master mason John Jackson. Above them, the small carvings in the panels are more refined. Many of the grotesques appear medieval. A strange mixture.

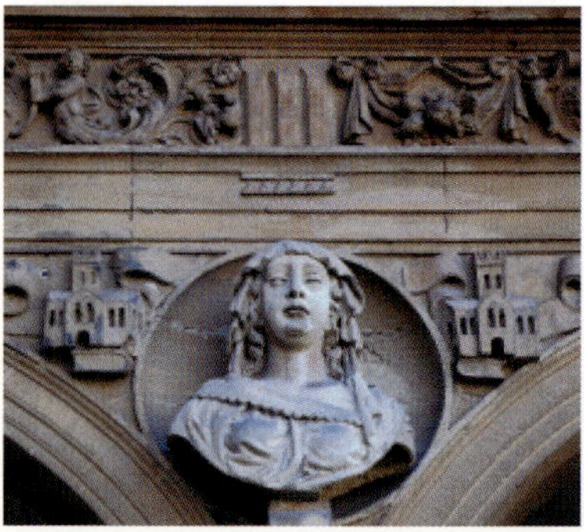

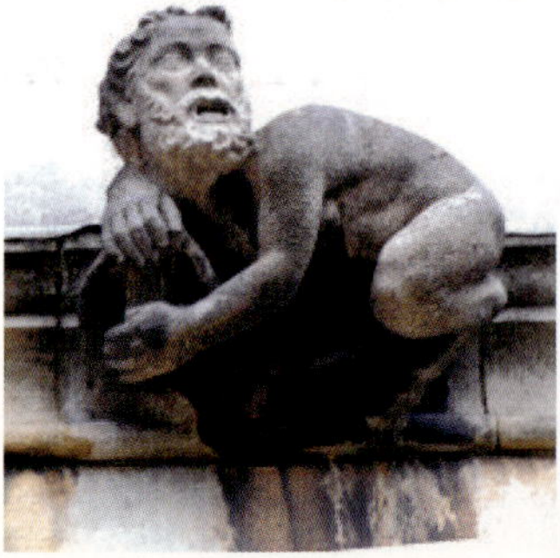

The Chapel

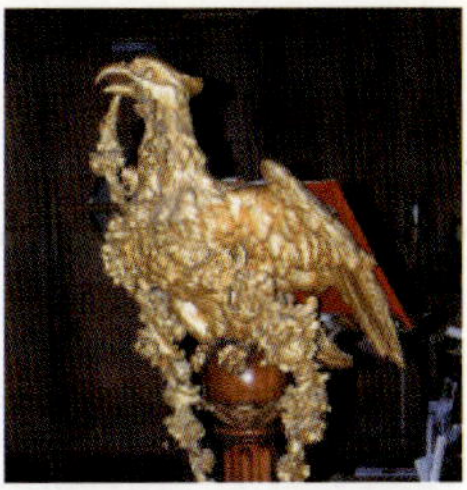

The college chapel is on the north side of Front Quad, with the entrance down a narrow passage. The first thing to admire in the interior of the chapel, a 19th-century restoration, is the **lectern** made in 1773, one of the most beautiful and elaborate in Oxford. An eagle holds in its beak a garland which twines around the supporting pillar

Baylie Chapel

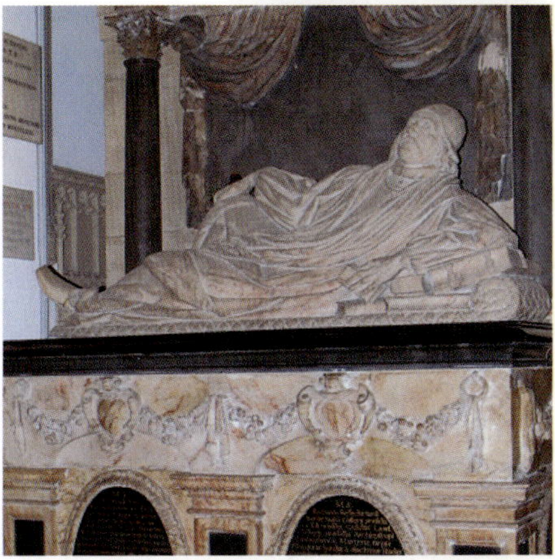

The main concentration of monuments is in this fan-vaulted chapel, built to receive the massive tomb and cheerful looking effigy of **Richard Baylie †1667,** President of the College and Vice-Chancellor of the University. The body of **Archbishop Laud †1645** perhaps the most influential of college presidents and University Chancellors, beheaded for Catholic tendencies, was reinterred here in 1663.

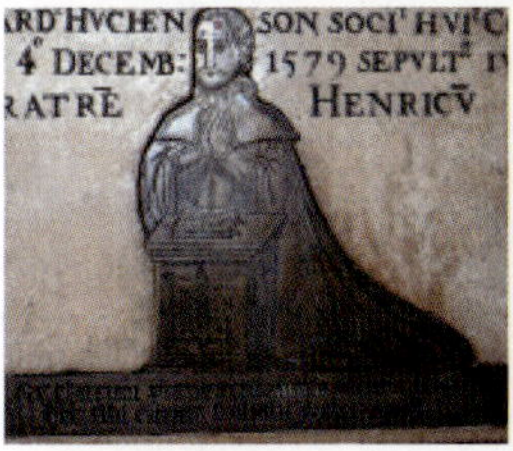

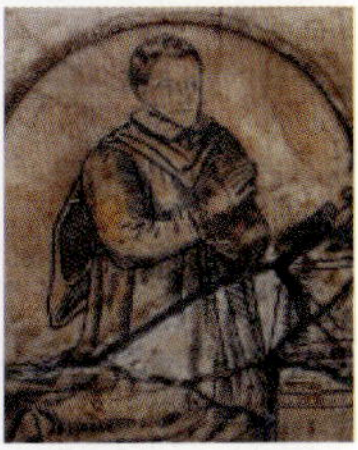

Among the Elizabethan wall brasses of kneeling figures is **Robert Harte †1571,** also a lovely incised panel to **John Wicksteed †1606**. The scholar memorial to **Ralph Hutchenson †1606** is typical of the period, with a painted half figure reading a book resting on a cushion. (Two similar memorials are on the right of the altar in the main chapel). In contrast, the splendid monument to **Sir William Paddy †1634,** an eminent physician, is an early example of accomplished Renaissance design. Notable among monuments is the beautiful black marble urn in a simple oval recess, to **Richard Rawlinson †1725** who donated his outstanding library to the Bodleian. Don't miss the beautiful relief of the Baptism in the lower part of the monument to **William Holmes †1748.**

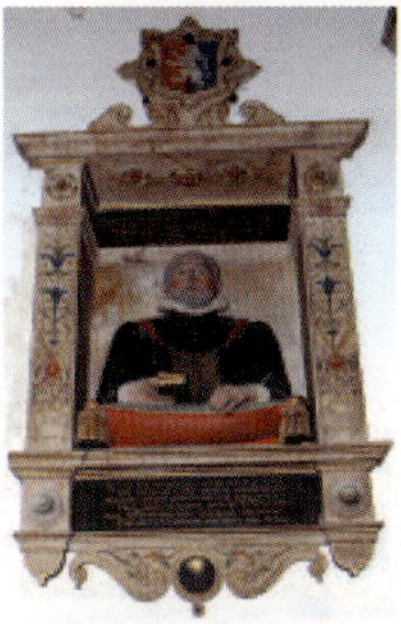

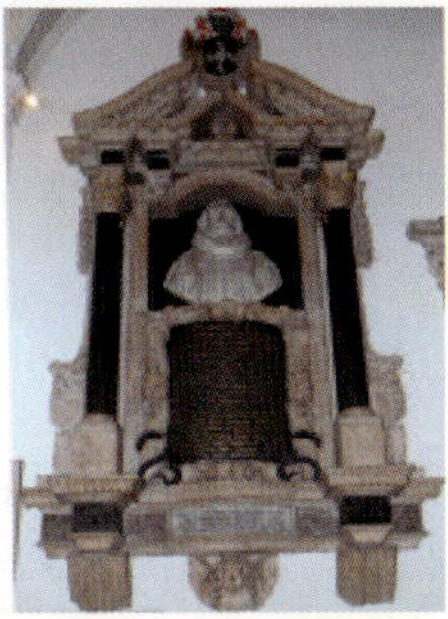

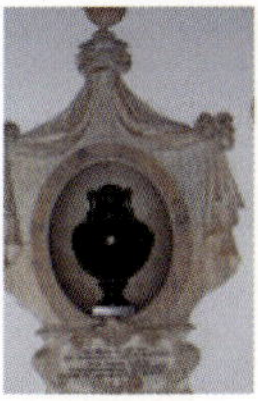

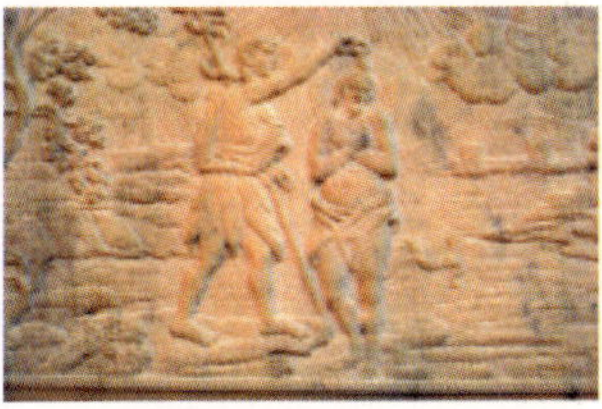

Sculpture elsewhere in the city

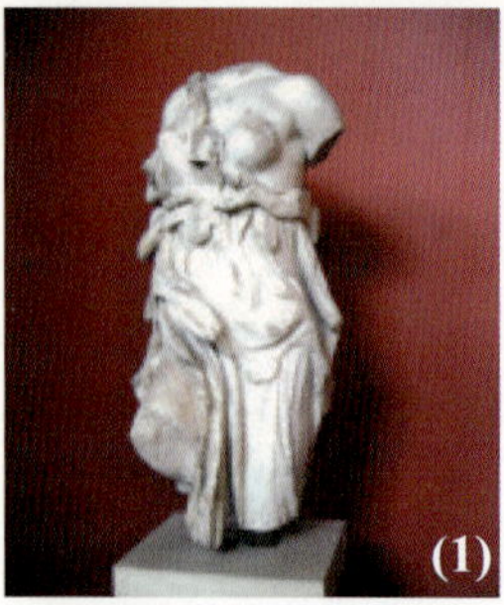
(1)

There are many more examples of sculpture and carvings to be found in Oxford.

The **Ashmolean Museum (1)** has an astonishing collection of statues from Egypt, Greece and Rome as well as cabinets full of fascinating and beautiful smaller pieces, votive offerings, tomb figures and domestic decorations. There is also a cast gallery with replicas of world famous examples. The wonderful **Pitt Rivers Museum (5)** has a huge collection of ethnological pieces which come within our broad definition of sculpture. Both these museums, although outside the scope of this booklet, should not be missed. Part of the university, but open, free, to the public every day except Mondays.

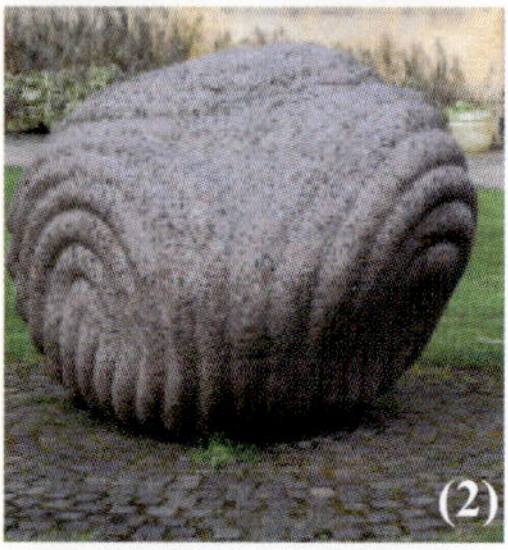
(2)

Elsewhere in the city, work by contemporary sculptors feature in exhibitions in the delightful **Turrill Sculpture Garden** at the rear of Summertown Public library. (Photograph **(3)** is a piece by Christopher Townsend.) There is a row of robust females, 'France, Germany, Italy, Spain' by *W.G. Nicholl* on the St Giles façade of the **Taylorian (4),** a large bronzes by *Barbara Hepwoth* at **St Catherine's (10)** and other modern works in the quad at **Nuffield College** including 'Flayed Stone' **(2)** by *Peter Randall-Page.* People interested in the work of *Eric Gill* will want to seek out his incised stations of the cross tucked away in **St Alban's Church (6-8)** Charles Street, East Oxford although they may have to attend a service on Sunday mornings to do so. There is a lovely life size figure 'Flore' by *Maillol* in the garden of the **Maison Française (11)** Norham Road.

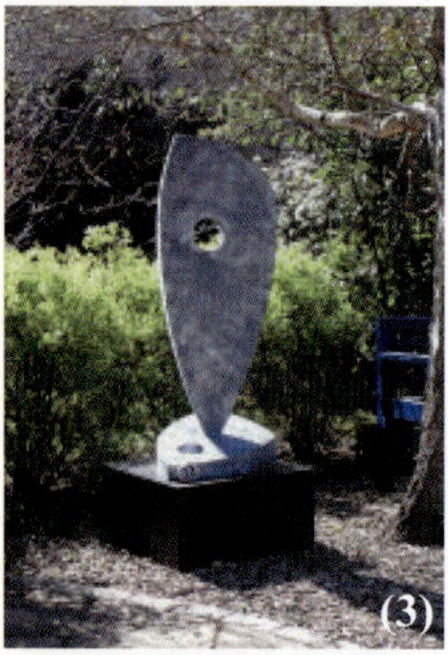
(3)

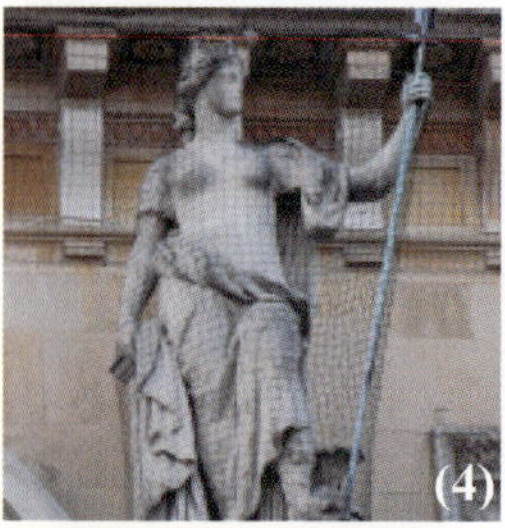
(4)

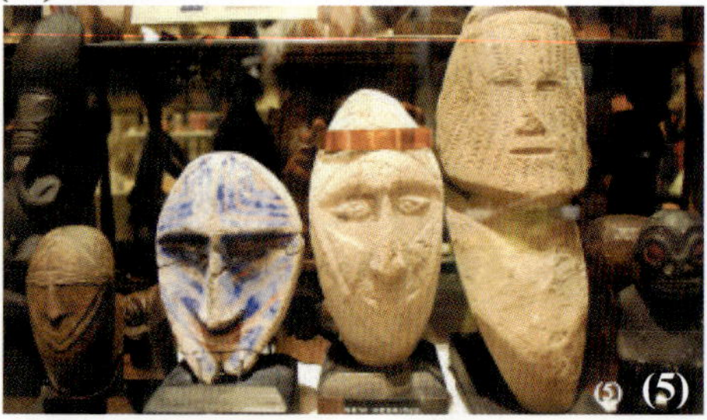
(5)

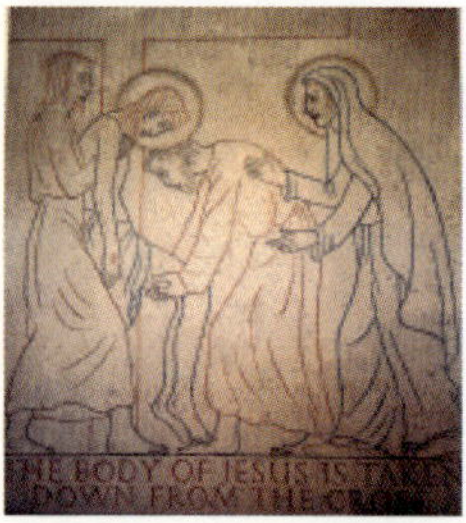

(6)

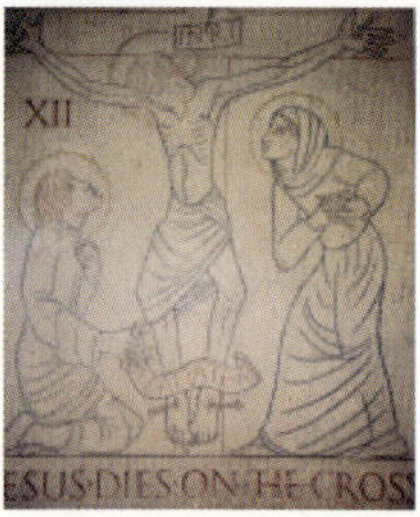

(7)

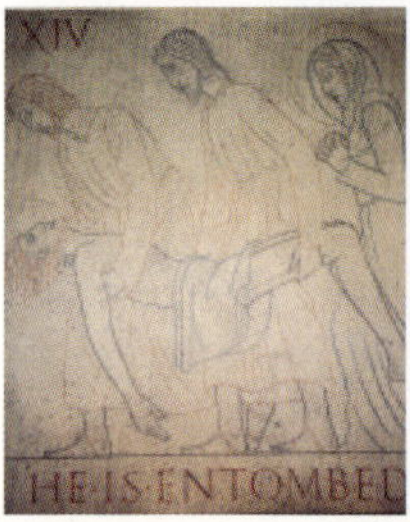

(8)

Glossary

Ballflower and crockets: 14c decoration to spire etc in globular, flower or leaf shapes.
Beakheads: Norman decorative motif of row of birds with prominent beaks.
Boss: Stone projection (often decorated) at junction of vaulting ribs.
Capital: Top of column, usually decorated, supporting arch or vault.
Cartouche: Memorial tablet with ornate frame enclosing inscription.
Classical: Style derived from ancient Greece or Rome.
Corbel: Block of stoneprojecting from wall to support roof truss,vault ribs etc
Keystone: Middle stone in arch or vault which weges them together.
Lierne vault: A late development of gothic vaulting introducing secondary ribs.
Pinnacles: Ornamental top to buttress or tower in conical form.
Reredos: Decorated wall behind altar.
Reformation: Here used for period after Henry VIII severed the link of the English church and Rome, leading to the dissolution of monasteries in the 1540s.
Renaissance: revival of Greek and Roman (Classical) styles.
Spandrel: Triangular space between arches,

Acknowledgements

Special thanks: To John Ashdown, David Eynon, Edward Evans, Liz Baird, and Joe, Melanie and Stewart at the Flying Press Witney. To the Master, President, Provost, Warden, Fellows and Bursars of Merton, All Souls, University, Magdalen, New, Wadham, St John's and Nuffield Colleges Oxford. To the Dean and Steward of Christ Church, the Vicars of St Mary's High Street and Iffley and St Alban's Church East Oxford. To the Librarian the Bodleian Library, and the Directors of the University Museum of Natural History and the Ashmolean Museum

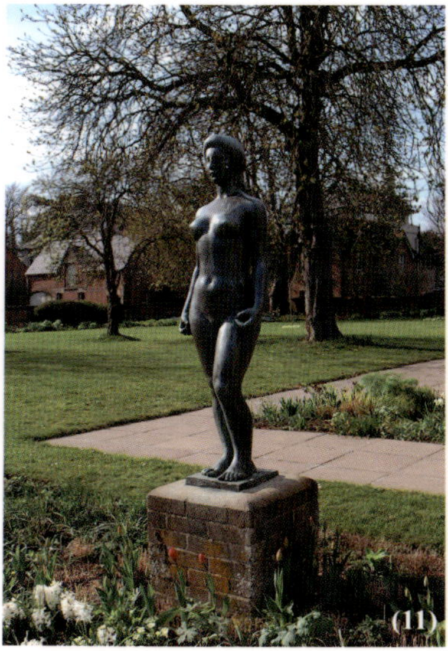
(11)

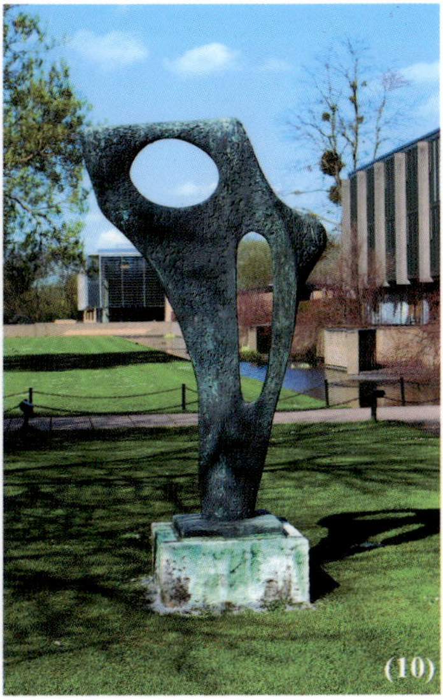
(10)

References

The Encyclopaedia of Oxford, edited by Christopher Hibbert and Antony Hibbert, Macmillan,1988.
Buildings of England - Oxfordshire, Jennifer Sherwood and Nikolaus Pevsner, Penguin, 1974.
City of Oxford, Royal Commission on Historic Monuments, HMSO.
Oxoniensia, Volume XI (1975).
Dictionary of British Art, Thames and Hudson,1985.
The statues in the court, Sarah Phibbs, University Museum of Natural History, 2008.
Monumental Brasses Herbert Macklin George Allen and Unwin, 1913.
Oxford, an architectural guide, Geoffrey Tyack, Oxford University Press, 1998.

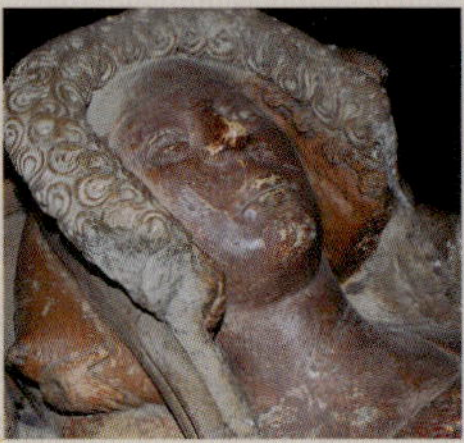

St Mary's Church Iffley

Schools Quadrangle

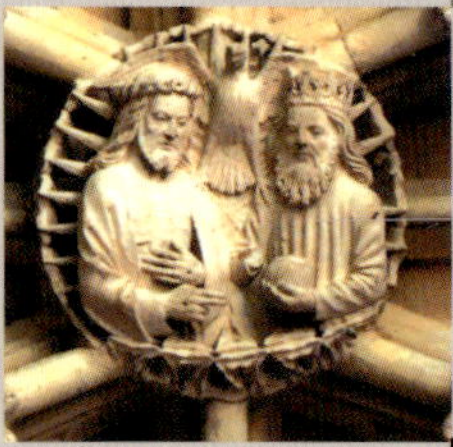

Merton College

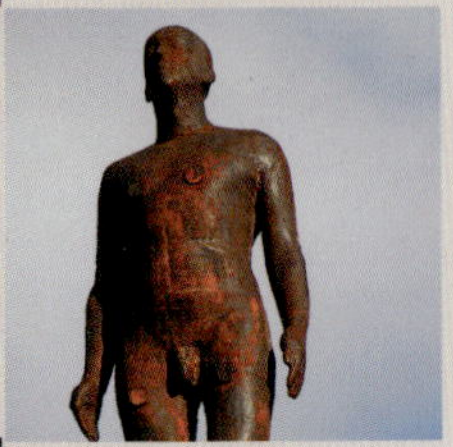

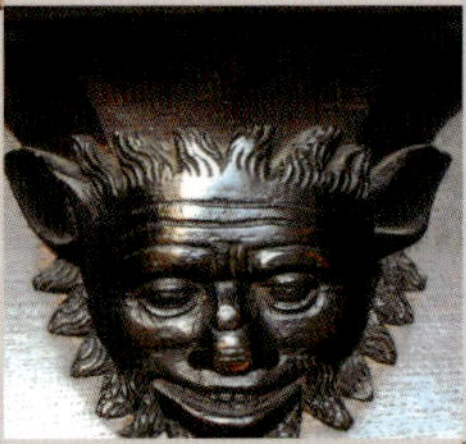

Christ Church Cathedral

All Souls College

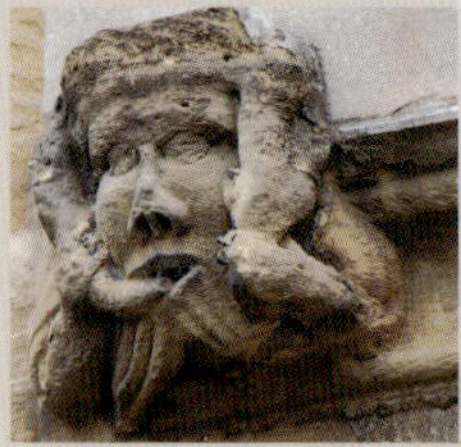

Trinity College

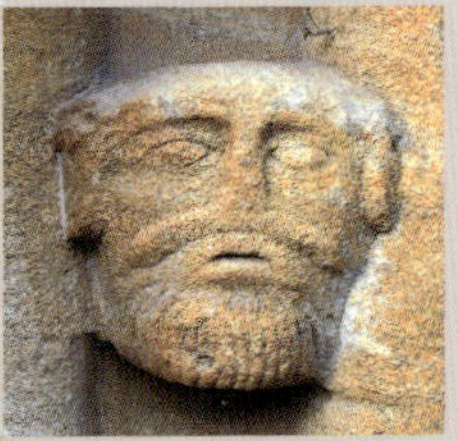

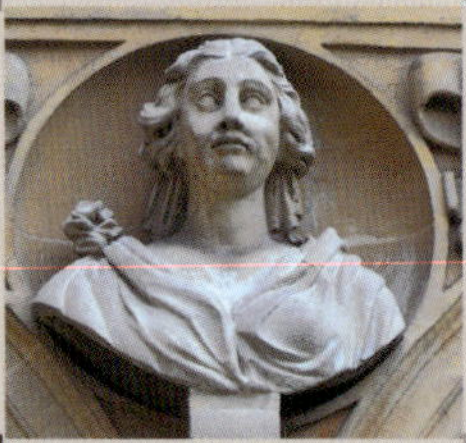

Magdalen College

St John's College

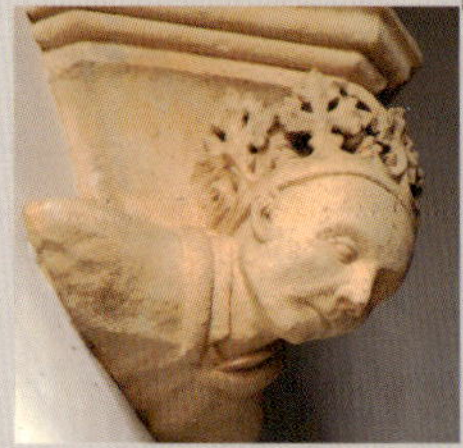

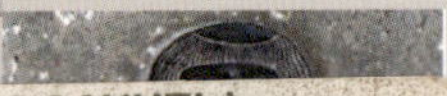

W
C

Heritage Tours
Publications

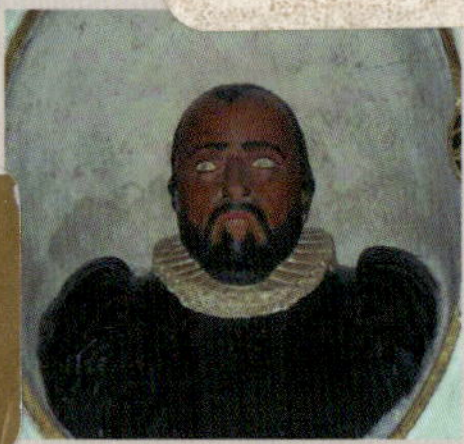

ISBN 978-1-874361-27-5